UML by Example

This step-by-step introduction to object-oriented software development is suitable for pedagogical training as well as for practicing software engineers seeking to add rigor to their techniques. The author presents seven complete case studies and several smaller examples documented in UML, derived from small software projects developed for and delivered to real users. These make use of a bridge process that instantiates generic aspects of software methods including iteration and traceability. The process and case studies are preceded by an overview of the object-oriented modeling artifact in UML on which the remainder of the book relies.

The bridge process presents a systematic approach for developing analysis models and unfolding these incrementally and iteratively through to design models and implementation. The process could be viewed as one instantiation of the unified software development process and has the potential of being scalable to large software problems. It also provides a model for organizing deliverables obtained throughout different phases of the software life cycle.

These case studies provide a medium for experimental use and act as templates that can be tailored by readers to fit their specific needs and circumstances.

Ghinwa Jalloul is Assistant Professor of Computer Science at the American University of Beirut, Lebanon, and the head of a parliamentarian committee of Information Technology at the Lebanese Parliament. In addition to her dedication to teaching and the development of academic programs, she is the founder of the Information and Technology Society in Lebanon and is widely published by a number of international forums.

UML by Example

Ghinwa Jalloul

American University of Beirut, Lebanon

CAMBRIDGE
UNIVERSITY PRESS

PUBLISHED BY THE PRESS SYNDICATE OF THE UNIVERSITY OF CAMBRIDGE
The Pitt Building, Trumpington Street, Cambridge, United Kingdom

CAMBRIDGE UNIVERSITY PRESS
The Edinburgh Building, Cambridge CB2 2RU, UK
40 West 20th Street, New York, NY 10011–4211, USA
477 Williamstown Road, Port Melbourne, VIC 3207, Australia
Ruiz de Alarcón 13, 28014 Madrid, Spain
Dock House, The Waterfront, Cape Town 8001, South Africa

http://www.cambridge.org

© Ghinwa Jalloul 2004

First published 2004

Printed in the United States of America

Typeface Stone Serif 9.5/12.5 pt.   *System* LaTeX 2_ε [TB]

A catalog record for this book is available from the British Library.

Library of Congress Cataloging in Publication Data
Jalloul, Ghinwa.
UML by example/Ghinwa Jalloul.
p. cm.
Includes bibliographical references and index.
ISBN 0-521-81051-5 (hc) – ISBN 0-521-00881-6 (pbk)
1. Application software – Development.   2. UML (Computer science)   3. Object-oriented
programming (Computer science)   I. Title.

QA76.76.D47J353   2003
005.1′7 – dc21   2003051228

ISBN 0 521 81051 5 hardback
ISBN 0 521 00881 6 paperback

To my family

Thank you. Your support, care, and understanding
have made this work possible.

Love, Ghinwa

Contents

List of Figures   *page* xiii
List of Bridge Process Patterns   xix
Preface   xxi

PART I

1. Modeling Concepts, Artifacts, and Relations   3
   1.1 Actor   3
   1.2 Use Case   7
   1.3 Use Case Model   11
   1.4 Primary Scenarios   19
   1.5 Secondary Scenarios   22
   1.6 Activity Diagram   25
   1.7 Objects and Classes   30
   1.8 Sequence and Collaboration Diagrams 39
   1.9 System Architecture   45
   1.10 Conclusion   47

2. Bridge: A Systematic Process Model   48
   2.1 An Overview of Process Models   48
   2.2 An Overview of the Bridge Process   50
   2.3 Inception Phase   53

	2.3.1	Determining User Requirements	55
	2.3.2	Determining Use Case Model	56
	2.3.3	Giving a Glossary	58
2.4	Elaboration		58
	2.4.1	Requirements Analysis	59
	2.4.2	Domain Analysis	63
	2.4.3	Subsystem Analysis	66
	2.4.4	Traceability	67
2.5	Construction Subphase 1		70
	2.5.1	Use Cases Revisited	70
	2.5.2	Dynamic Modeling	71
	2.5.3	Detailed Object Design	71
	2.5.4	Traceability	77
2.6	Construction Subphase 2		78
2.7	Conclusion		79

PART II

3. Reservations Online: Case Study 1   83
3.1	Inception		83
	3.1.1	User Requirements	83
	3.1.2	Use Case Model (version 1)	84
3.2	Elaboration		87
	3.2.1	Requirements Analysis	87
	3.2.2	Domain Analysis: Deriving the Initial Object Model	95
	3.2.3	Software Systems Architecture (version 1)	101
	3.2.4	Traceability	103
3.3	Construction		113
	3.3.1	Use Case (version 2)	113
	3.3.2	Dynamic Modeling (Sequence and Collaboration Diagrams)	114
	3.3.3	Object Design	120
	3.3.4	Revisiting the Subsystem Model	124
3.4	Construction/Implementation		124

4. Web Page Maker: Case Study 2   130
    4.1   Inception   130
          4.1.1 User Requirements   130
          4.1.2 Use Case Model (version 1)   131
    4.2   Elaboration   133
          4.2.1 Requirements Analysis   134
          4.2.2 Domain Analysis: Deriving the Initial Object
                 Model   141
          4.2.3 Software Systems Architecture (version 1)   147
          4.2.4 Traceability   149
    4.3   Construction   157
          4.3.1 Use Case (version 2)   157
          4.3.2 Dynamic Modeling: Sequence and Collaboration
                 Diagrams   158
          4.3.3 Object Design   164
          4.3.4 Revisiting Subsystem Model   166
    4.4   Construction/Implementation   166

PART III

5. Simulating a Robot Arm: Case Study 3   171
    5.1   Inception   172
          5.1.1 User Requirements   172
          5.1.2 Use Case Model (version 1)   174
    5.2   Elaboration   175
          5.2.1 Requirements Analysis   175
          5.2.2 Domain Analysis: Deriving the Initial Object
                 Model   180
          5.2.3 Software Systems Architecture (version 1)   182
          5.2.4 Traceability   183
    5.3   Construction   184
          5.3.1 Use Case (version 2)   184
          5.3.2 Dynamic Modeling: Sequence and Collaboration
                 Diagrams   185
          5.3.3 Object Design   188
    5.4   Construction/Implementation   188

6.   Math Tutor: Case Study 4   192
   6.1   Inception   193
         6.1.1 User Requirements   193
         6.1.2 Use Case Model (version 1)   194
   6.2   Elaboration   194
         6.2.1 Requirements Analysis   194
         6.2.2 Domain Analysis: Deriving the Initial Object
                Model   197
         6.2.3 Software Systems Architecture (version 1)   199
         6.2.4 Traceability   200
   6.3   Construction   201
         6.3.1 Use Case (version 2)   201
         6.3.2 Dynamic Modeling: Sequence and Collaboration
                Diagrams   202
         6.3.3 Object Design   205
   6.4   Construction/Implementation   206

7.   Distribution Case: Case Study 5   208
   7.1   Inception   209
         7.1.1 User Requirements   209
         7.1.2 Use Case Model (version 1)   213
   7.2   Elaboration   213
         7.2.1 Requirements Analysis   213
         7.2.2 Domain Analysis: Deriving the Initial Object
                Model   224
         7.2.3 Software Systems Architecture (version 1)   225
         7.2.4 Traceability   225
   7.3   Construction   227
         7.3.1 Use Case (version 2)   227
         7.3.2 Dynamic Modeling: Sequence and Collaboration
                Diagrams   228
         7.3.3 Object Design   233

Appendix A: Recommended Practice   235

Bibliography   241
Index   243

Figures

ACTIVITY DIAGRAMS

1-31	Activity diagram for a single send session of an online chat system	*page* 25
1-32	Activity diagram for a complete chat session	26
1-33	Activity diagram for a password-based transaction	27
1-34	Activity diagram for a university probation system	28
1-35	Activity diagram for a person watching television	29
1-36	Activity diagram for a computer system	30
3-2	Starting Tours Online	91
3-3	Reserving	92
3-4	Viewing information	93
3-5	Canceling	93
3-6	Administrate	94
3-7	Complaining	94
3-10	Trace of Starting activity from Figure 3-2	104
3-11	Trace of Reserving activity in Figure 3-3	105
3-12	Trace of Viewing Information activity in Figure 3-4	106
3-13	Trace of Canceling activity in Figure 3-5	106
3-14	Trace of Administrate activity in Figure 3-6	107
3-15	Trace of Complaining activity in Figure 3-7	108
4-2	Page Maker design home page	137

4-3	Page Maker create home page	139
4-5	Page Maker upload home page	140
4-6	Page Maker delete home page	140
5-2	Robot arm Get Help	177
5-3	Robot arm Lift an Object	178
5-4	Robot arm Test	180
6-2	Tutor Takes Consecutive Lesson activity	196
6-3	Tutor Chooses to Practice activity	197
7-2	Distribution Order Management activity	220
7-3	Distribution Customer Contact Info activity	221
7-4	Distribution Vendor Contact Info activity	222
7-5	Distribution Product Info activity	223
7-6	Distribution Warehouse Contact Info activity	223

ACTORS

1-1	Actors of a real estate system	4
1-2	Actors of a reseller company	4
1-3	Actors of a rent-a-car system	5
1-4	An employee as a customer	6
1-5	Managers of an IT department	7

COLLABORATION DIAGRAMS

1-56	Collaboration diagram of a bookstore	44
1-57	Collaboration diagram of an ATM system	44
3-19	Tours Online Starting activity collaboration diagram	115
3-21	Tours Online Reserving collaboration diagram	116
3-23	Tours Online Viewing Information collaboration diagram	117
3-25	Tours Online Canceling a Reservation collaboration diagram	118
3-27	Tours Online Administrate collaboration diagram	119
3-29	Tours Online Registering a Complaint collaboration diagram	120
4-17	Page Maker Design Home Page collaboration diagram	159
4-19	Page Maker Create Home Page collaboration diagram	160
4-21	Page Maker Create Home Page collaboration diagram	161
4-23	Page Maker Upload Home Page collaboration diagram	162
4-25	Page Maker Delete Home Page collaboration diagram	163
5-9	Robot arm Get Help collaboration diagram	185

5-11	Robot arm Lift an Object collaboration diagram	187
5-13	Robot arm Test collaboration diagram	188
6-8	Tutor Takes Consecutive Lessons collaboration diagram	203
6-10	Tutor Chooses to Practice collaboration diagram	205
7-10	Order Management collaboration diagram	228
7-12	Customer Contact Info collaboration diagram	229
7-14	Vendor Contact Info collaboration diagram	230
7-16	Product Info collaboration diagram	231
7-18	Warehouse Contact Info collaboration diagram	232

DESCRIPTIONS

Description 3-1	Tours Online user requirements	84
Description 3-2	Tours Online glossary of actors	86
Description 3-3	Tours Online subsystems description	102
Description 4-1	Page Maker user requirements	131
Description 4-2	Page Maker glossary of actors	133
Description 4-3	Page Maker subsystems description	148
Description 5-1	Robot arm user requirements	172
Description 5-2	Robot arm glossary of technical terms	173
Description 5-3	Robot arm subsystems description	182
Description 6-1	Tutor user requirements	193
Description 6-2	Tutor subsystems description	199
Description 7-1	Distribution user requirements	209

OBJECT MODELS

1-37	Classes of a rent-a-car system	31
1-38	Classes of a library system	31
1-39	Book and Librarian classes with attributes	32
1-40	Book and Librarian classes with operations	33
1-41	Parameterized List class	33
1-42	One-to-one association	34
1-43	One-to-many association	34
1-44	Self-association in a chat system	35
1-45	Many-to-many association in a reservation system	36
1-46	Company consists of one-to-many branches	36
1-47	Aggregation among several classes	36
1-48	An employee is a client	37

1-49	Buyer, Seller, and Broker are Financial Market Persons	38
1-50	Object model of a school database	39
1-51	Joke-teller object model	40
2-8	An example of a design of a one-to-one association	72
2-9	A one-to-many association	73
2-10	Design of a one-to-many association	73
2-11	A many-to-many association	74
2-12	Design of a many-to-many association	74
2-13	An aggregation	75
2-14	Design of an aggregation relation	75
2-15	University student association	76
2-16	Design of university student association	76
3-8	Tours Online object model	95
3-30	Tours Online object design model	121
3-32	Tours Online reverse engineering object design model	127
4-7	Page Maker object initial model	141
4-26	Page Maker object design model	164
5-14	Robot arm object design model	189
5-15	Robot arm reverse engineering object model	190
6-4	Tutor object model	198
6-11	Tutor object design model	206
7-7	Distribution object model	224
7-19	Distribution object design model	233

SEQUENCE DIAGRAMS

1-52	Model sequence diagram	41
1-53	Model sequence diagram	41
1-54	Bookstore inventory sequence diagram	42
1-55	Sequence diagram of buying a property	43
2-17	A sequence diagram from a reservation system	76
3-18	Tours Online Starting sequence diagram	115
3-20	Tours Online Reserving activity sequence diagram	116
3-22	Tours Online Viewing Information sequence diagram	117
3-24	Tours Online Canceling a Reservation sequence diagram	117
3-26	Tours Online Administrate sequence diagram	118
3-28	Tours Online Registering a Complaint sequence diagram	119
4-16	Tours Online Design Home Page sequence diagram	159
4-17	Design Home Page collaboration diagram	159
4-18	Page Maker Create the Home Page sequence diagram	160
4-20	Page Maker Preview Home Page sequence diagram	161

4-22   Page Maker Upload Home Page sequence diagram   162
4-24   Page Maker Delete Home Page sequence diagram   163
5-8   Robot arm Get Help sequence diagram   185
5-10   Robot arm Lift an Object sequence diagram   186
5-12   Robot arm Test sequence diagram   187
6-7   Tutor Takes Consecutive Lessons sequence diagram   202
6-9   Tutor Chooses to Practice sequence diagram   204
7-9   Order Management sequence diagram   228
7-11   Customer Contact Info sequence diagram   229
7-13   Vendor Contact Info sequence diagram   230
7-15   Product Info sequence diagram   231
7-17   Distribution Warehouse Contact Info sequence diagram   232

SUBSYSTEM MODEL

1-58   Site ordering subsystem model   46
1-59   Consulting company subsystem model   46
3-9   Tours Online subsystem model   101
4-8   Page Maker subsystem model   147
4-27   Page Maker subsystem model   167
5-6   Robot arm subsystem model   182
6-5   Tutor subsystem model   199

TRACEABILITY

3-10   Trace of Starting activity from Figure 3-2   104
3-11   Trace of Reserving activity in Figure 3-3   105
3-12   Trace of Viewing Information activity in Figure 3-4   106
3-13   Trace of Canceling activity in Figure 3-5   106
3-14   Trace of Administrate activity in Figure 3-6   107
3-15   Trace of Complaining activity in Figure 3-7   108
3-16   Tours Online object map to subsystem model   111
3-31   Tours Online object map to subsystem model (version 2) 125
4-9   Page Maker trace of Design Home Page activity in Figure 4-2   149
4-10   Page Maker trace of Create Home Page activity in Figure 4-3   150
4-11   Page Maker trace of Preview Home Page activity in
       Figure 4-4   151
4-12   Page Maker trace of Upload Home Page activity in
       Figure 4-5   151
4-13   Page Maker trace Delete Home Page activity in Figure 4-6   152

4-14   Page Maker object map to subsystem model   155
4-27   Page Maker object map to subsystem model (version 2)   167

USE CASES AND MODELS

1-6   Use cases of a real estate property   8
1-7   Use cases of an online chat system   8
1-8   Use cases of a university registration system   8
1-9   Boat purchase   9
1-10   Search activity   10
1-11   Bookstore inventory system   11
1-12   Customer orders books   12
1-13   ATM machine gives money   12
1-14   Two musical devices playing music   13
1-15   The three tasks of an interior designer   14
1-16   Online chat system use case model   14
1-17   Use case model of a reseller company   15
1-18   School database use case model   16
1-19   Use case model of a computer game   17
1-20   User interface   18
1-21   Output interface   18
1-22   Use case model of a university probation system   19
3-1   Use case model of Tours Online   86
3-17   Tours Online use case model (version 2)   113
4-1   Page Maker use case model   133
4-15   Page Maker use case model (version 2)   157
5-1   Robot arm use case model   174
5-7   Robot arm use case model (version 2)   184
6-1   Tutor use case model   194
6-6   Tutor use case model (version 2)   201
7-1   Distribution use case model   214
7-8   Distribution use case model (version 2)   227

Bridge Process Patterns

FIGURES

2-1	A snapshot of the bridge process	*page* 51
2-2	A linear view of the bridge process model	52
2-3	Deliverables of bridge process	53
2-5	Deliverables of the elaboration phase	59
2-7	Traceability model	68

PATTERNS

Pattern 2-1	Inception phase	54
Pattern 2-2	Requirement analysis	60
Pattern 2-3	Requirements analysis (simplified version)	61
Pattern 2-4	Domain analysis	64
Pattern 2-5	Subsystem analysis	66

Preface

This book is meant to serve pedagogical and practical purposes by presenting a process called *Bridge*, which instantiates generic aspects of software methods including iteration and traceability. It also presents seven case studies documented in Unified Modeling Language (UML). The process and case studies are preceded by an overview of object-oriented modeling artifacts that act as a background for developing the concepts in the process and for presenting the case studies.

The book is appealing for a variety of readers because it provides a comprehensive view of modeling artifacts and how they fit together in an iterative context to provide working solutions. The approach that it adopts has the advantage of cutting down the learning curve and of bridging the gap between theory and practice. Readers will learn from the experience of other developments. The underlying theme is that a considerable amount of learning is achieved through practical applications of the theories involved; teaching object-oriented development could be made more effective by relying on documented practices.

This book is adequate for an introduction to object-oriented software development for pedagogical, training, and practical purposes. The first part is appropriate for a course on object-oriented development, whereas the second part on the case studies provides the meat for technical training. In addition, we believe that novices in practical contexts would benefit from this book, which cuts down the learning curve. Software engineers seeking to add rigor to their techniques would also find this book useful.

The introductory chapter describes modeling artifacts on which the remainder of the book relies. The artifacts are expressed in UML. This chapter relies heavily on examples derived from a large number of case studies, which makes it useful for readers interested in getting a quick introduction on object-oriented and UML modeling concepts, artifacts, and notation.

The bridge process and accompanying case studies present and disseminate instances of applications of principles and practice of object-oriented development. These also illustrate the use of UML for expressing software models and how these models can be mapped to implementations.

The bridge process presents a systematic approach for developing analysis models and unfolding these, incrementally and iteratively, on through to design models and implementation. The process could be viewed as one instantiation of the unified software development process and has the potential of being scalable to large software problems. It also provides a model for organizing deliverables obtained throughout different phases of the software life cycle and acts as a background for detailing the development of two case studies.

The detailed case studies provide packages that students and instructors can use for pedagogical and training advantage. In serving pedagogical and training purposes, the detailed specifications of two case studies demonstrate how solutions can be reached systematically and how generic aspects in developing software can be instantiated. Consequently, these agree with the observation that the primary barriers to valid development could be controlled and their effects diminished.

Because many elements of development are driven by the expertise of developers, rather than laboring to produce detailed solutions throughout, the book asserts that there is "no silver bullet," so the remaining case studies are presented as reached by developers. These as-is case studies provide a basket for experimental use and act as potentially replicable practices that can be exploited by readers after suitable tailoring to fit their specific needs and circumstances.

WHY THIS BOOK

A key challenge of writing this book was the identification of an interesting range of software solutions to practical software problems. Also, the size of the problems was yet another challenge that required much attention. Case studies typically emerge from real-world examples or model the same. Real problems are large and complex, which makes them inappropriate to use for explaining concepts, not to mention that detailed documents on such models are of commercial value that is not publicly available. To give the case studies in this book real flavor, some of the case studies were developed for small businesses and advanced versions of the described versions are now operational. Also, we chose to present small problems that can be modeled and presented within the context of a single book and can be used to relay object-oriented development concepts. Despite their size, the solutions are enticing because these cover all phases of development.

Another challenge is the method of development and presentation of the case studies to maximize the benefit. This has motivated the development of the bridge process model. Methodologies and processes are generic, leaving many decisions to the expertise and judgment of involved workers. By and large, these provide general directives leaving many details undefined, which prevents the immediate application of methodology by working through an example. One generic aspect is iteration. None of the existing methodologies or processes specify when or how iteration is to be performed. Another generic aspect is achieving traceability among various deliverables of the development process. Because of the complexity of deliverables, stepwise traceability could be tedious, and the iteration through the deliverables to ensure correctness of the final product is uncontrollable. Whereas for educational or training purposes, a presentation of a case study would have to explain the role of these deliverables, and how these trace from one another and contribute to the complete development.

These challenges were identified as a result of our experience in teaching object-oriented development for more than five years; we found that learning by example is one theme whose potential is hard to achieve in the context of object-oriented development. There is a lack of thorough case studies and modeling examples, which has been expressed as a need in several occasions and in various object-oriented contexts. The published examples are by and large classical in the sense that they focus on the same problems. Additionally, these are presented to demonstrate the use of notation or a single concept independent of the context of development. In teaching object-oriented software engineering, the lack of thorough case studies proved to be a severe discrepancy when we needed to demonstrate how the concepts could be utilized collaboratively throughout development. Because object-oriented models are based on a variety of interrelated artifacts that have temporal and iterative dependencies, presenting concepts independently fell short of relaying the role and contribution of the artifact to the development process.

We hope that we have been able to address these key challenges in writing this book.

CONTENTS

The book consists of seven chapters organized into three parts. The first chapter is the introduction to modeling artifacts, the second chapter introduces the bridge process, and the remaining chapters contain the case studies. Following is the outline of the book.

Part I: Introduction

This part introduces object-oriented modeling artifacts and the layout and the approaches that will be followed in presenting the detailed case studies.

- **Chapter 1: Modeling Concepts, Artifacts, and Relations**
  This chapter introduces modeling concepts and artifacts including use cases, classes, objects, subsystems, state diagrams, and activity diagrams. The objective is to familiarize readers with object-oriented modeling artifacts and set the framework for the remainder of the book.

- **Chapter 2: Bridge: A Systematic Process Model**
  This chapter describes a multidimensional, multiiterative process for developing software. The process organizes deliverables of the analysis, design, and implementation phases into the inception, elaboration, and construction phases. Based on this organization the process allows for specification of requirements in terms of the three dimensions of system architecture: use case model, object model, and software architecture model. It involves continual incremental unfolding of these models, in which each increment contributes to solve the problem and in many ways with the involvement and the judgment of the analyst. The process relies heavily on dynamic modeling, in particular, and activity diagrams to achieve traceability among requirements' artifacts. Gradually it gives a comprehensive multidimensional analysis, design and implementation models integrated into the inception, and elaboration and construction phases of development.

Part II: Detailed Case Studies

- **Chapter 3: Reservations Online: Case Study 1**
  Work on this case study was motivated by an anticipated need of travel agencies to improve their sales by making their products, namely tours, directly accessible to their client base. Customers as well as travel agents and their employees would be able to view data on tours and to make reservations if desired. The current development focuses on travel agencies but it could be viewed as one instantiation of a general application framework that handles reservations in general, such as hotel, car, and so forth.

- **Chapter 4: Web Page Maker: Case Study 2**
  Work on this case study was motivated by the need to provide a tool to simplify the development of personal web pages and it was requested by an ISP for its clients. The case study is detailed based on the bridge process.

Part III: As-is Case Studies

This part presents a suite of case studies as they were developed. The presentation of these case studies follows the same layout described in the introduction.

- **Chapter 5: Simulating a Robot Arm: Case Study 3**
  This case study provides a design for simulating a robot arm.

- **Chapter 6: Math Tutor: Case Study 4**
  Math tutor is an application that educates and trains students in lower level classes in mathematics. The application supports three levels (low, medium, and high) of competency, where each level contains several stages that students have to complete to move across levels.

- **Chapter 7: Distribution Case: Case Study 5**
  This case study was developed for a reseller of goods. The company obtains its products from a vendor and resells them to a customer. The basic requirement is a database to keep track of specific information concerning the various vendors, customers, and warehouses, as well as a product database.

ACKNOWLEDGMENTS

There are a number of people without whom this work would not have been possible. My thanks are to my students, whose participation with applying the bridge process and experimenting with it had made this possible. Special thanks to Mira Al Khatib, my graduate assistant, whose support and help has been precious. Also thanks to my secretary Zeina Jalloul for her support.

Also my biggest thanks is to my family whose loving support and patience has been essential to make this book possible.

Part I

Modeling Artifacts and Bridge Process

*This part introduces modeling artifacts that are used to express architectures in terms of uses cases and objects. The second chapter introduces the **bridge** process.*

Chapter 1

Modeling Concepts, Artifacts, and Relations

This chapter introduces modeling concepts, artifacts, relations, and the corresponding graphical representations. It relies on examples expressed in UML graphical notation. Most of the examples introduced are built upon in subsequent chapters to give thorough examples.

1. ACTOR

An ***actor*** is something or someone that interacts with the target system to produce an observable result. An actor falls on the boundary of the system. Actors model the roles of real users using the system for different purposes or systems that interact with the software system, such as a border system that receives input from the main system. A system may have one or more actors. A real user that has different roles with respect to uses of a system could be modeled by more than one actor.

Classes are the corresponding implementation concepts of actors. An actor class may have features and attributes like any other class.

Following is the UML stick-person notation for representing actors that model real users. A classlike representation is used to model nonreal users. Each actor is given a name that is selected to reflect the role that an actor models.

Actor's Name
Actor

Figure 1-1 shows three actors: *Broker, Buyer,* and *Seller* of a real estate system.

Broker is an actor who is the owner of the system and can use the system to update data on real estate property. *Buyer* and *Seller* are actors that can use the system to browse through the available property list and place purchase orders or sale requests. Note that *Broker, Buyer,* and *Seller* could be roles for a single real user who is the owner of the real estate software. The same actors may represent different real users for an Internet real estate system where buyers and sellers can interact with the software through the web or other means to place a purchase order or to post a real estate property for sale.

Figure 1-2 shows three actors, *Warehouse Employee, Customer,* and *Vendor,* of a software solution for a company that resells goods. It obtains the products from vendors and resells to customers.

Warehouse Employee is the active user of the system who can update data on goods for all warehouses. *Vendors* are passive actors who receive requests from *Customer* actors through the system and respond to these requests when activated by the *Warehouse Employee.*

Broker   Buyer   Seller
***Figure 1-1.* Actors of a real estate system**

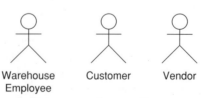

Warehouse   Customer   Vendor
Employee
***Figure 1-2.* Actors of a reseller company**

Actor Categories

In general, actors fall into two categories: **Active** actors, who initiate interactions with a system, such as persons who use the system to perform an activity, and **passive** actors, who receive requests or input from a system and are activated by these to carry an activity.

For example, *Warehouse Employee* actor of Figure 1-2 is an active actor because he issues requests to a system. *Vendor* is a passive actor because he responds to requests from the system when processed by *Warehouse Employee* actor. Figure 1-3 shows two active actors and one passive actor: *Employee*, *Customer*, and *Accounting System* of an online rent-a-car software system.

The system permits users to make online reservations of cars. Rental charges are computed by a boundary accounting system. Both *Employee* and *Customer* are active actors. *Employee* is an actor in charge of the reservation system and *Customer* is an actor that uses the system to effect a reservation. *Employee* and *Customer* are two different actors because they stand for two different roles. The accounting system is a passive actor that receives the details of the reservation and computes the corresponding rental charges. Note the stick-person representation of real users versus the classlike representation of a nonreal actor.

Generalization among Actors

Actors may be related by a **generalization relationship**. Specialization relation is the opposite of generalization relation, and it is similar to inheritance relation among classes:

An actor A is a generalization of an actor B (B inherits A) whenever B and A are related by the is-a relation as follows: B is-a A. This permits B to assume the same roles modeled by actor A, whereas actor A need not necessarily play the same roles as B. A is the parent actor, and B is the descendant actor.

Generalization is a one-way transitive relation. Consequently, if actor A is a generalization of an actor B and B is a generalization of an actor C, then A is a generalization of actor C and consequently actor C can assume the same roles modeled by A.

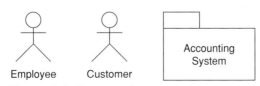

Figure 1-3. **Actors of a rent-a-car system**

The following is a template of the generalization relation between two actors.

Actor's generalization

Figure 1-4 shows an application of generalization relation to *Customer* and *Employee* actors of a rent-a-car system. An employee may be a customer and use the system to order a car but a customer is not necessarily an employee.

Figure 1-5 shows another example of a generalization relation where one actor could have one or more descendants. Actors *System Manager* and *Information Security Manager* are descendants of actor *IT Manager*; both are IT managers but an IT manager is not necessarily a specialized manager.

An actor could be a parent of more than one actor – each of its descendants could assume roles modeled by the parent actor.

Customer

Employee

Figure 1-4. An employee as a customer

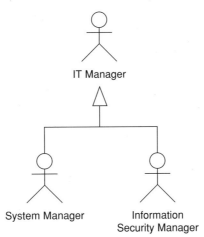

Figure 1-5. Managers of an IT department

2. USE CASE

A ***use case*** is one instance of how an actor would use a software system to activate a business function that is a service offered by the system and to produce a result. With use cases it is possible to specify all services offered to users by the system when use cases are related to actors these directly specify functionality of the system.

A use case is modeled with an oval and a descriptive name string that describes its functions. The following is the notation for modeling a ***use case***.

Name of Use Case
Use case

Use cases typically stand for verb phrases that can be derived from user requirements and from possible uses of the system by actors.

Figure 1-6 shows three use cases of a real estate property: *Browse, Sell a Property*, and *Buy a Property*. Each of these use cases indicates a single service provided by the system. The three reflect the main functionality of the real estate property system. *Browse* permits a user to browse existing data of real estate, *Sell a Property* permits a user to add real estate to the existing data, and *Buy a Property* permits a user to place a purchase order.

Figure 1-7 shows an example of four use cases of an online chat system: *Add User, Remove User, Receive Message,* and *Send Message.* The system is designed so that it allows users to start chatting from within a chat room. A user can enter a

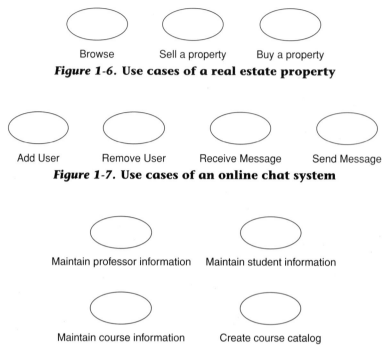

Figure 1-6. **Use cases of a real estate property**

Figure 1-7. **Use cases of an online chat system**

Figure 1-8. **Use cases of a university registration system**

session by logging into the chat room; chatting involves sending and receiving messages from other logged in users. A user can terminate a chat session by removing himself from the chat room. Each of the four use cases models one service that could be utilized by users. The *Add User* and *Remove User* use cases allow a chat user to add or remove himself from the chat room. The *Receive Message* and *Send Message* use cases allow a chat client to communicate with other chat clients.

Figure 1-8 shows another example of use cases of a university registration system that permits registering students in courses taught by professors. The *Maintain Course Information* and *Create Course Catalog* use cases model services offered by the system to the registrar office to update a course content or to add a new course in the system. The *Maintain Professor Information* and *Maintain Student Information* use cases model services of the system that permit the registrar office to update the information regarding university's professors or students.

Use cases could be used to model general services of a system or to model simple atomic actions. It all depends on the intended level of granularity to be reached by a system analyst during the analysis stage.

Extend Relationship

Use cases may be related by an ***extend relation***. An extend relationship is a generalization relationship where one use case extends another use case by adding actions to it.

The following is a template of the extend relation between use cases.

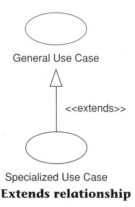

General Use Case

<<extends>>

Specialized Use Case
Extends relationship

In the boat-purchase example (Figure 1-9), an *extends* relation is applied to two use cases, *Signing Boat Purchase Contract* and *Signing Insurance Policy*, because signing an insurance policy is a part of, and typically precedes, signing a purchase contract.

In Figure 1-10, the use case *Search* extends *Browse* because every search, when it commences, requires a browsing activity.

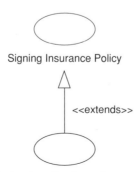

Signing Insurance Policy

<<extends>>

Signing Boat Purchase Contract
Figure 1-9. **Boat purchase**

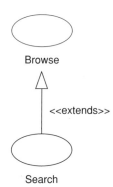

Figure 1-10. Search activity

Uses Relationship

Use cases may be related by a ***uses relation***. ***Uses*** is a generalization relationship where one use case uses another use case indicating that, as part of the specialized use case, the behavior of the general use case will also be included.

The following is a template of uses relation between use cases.

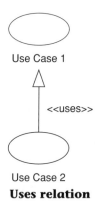

Uses relation

The *uses* relation is different from the *extends* relation. In fact, the *extends* relationship involves inheritance because the specialized use case is a subset of the general one. In the *uses* relation, the two use cases might not have any kind of inheritance but one still uses the other for a specific purpose.

In the bookstore inventory system, we have the *Locates Book* use case that uses the *Gives Price* use case. In this case the ***uses*** relation is more appropriate than the ***extends*** relation because whenever a book is located it has to return the price of the item and, hence, it uses the use case *Gives Price*. This is modeled in Figure 1-11.

Figure 1-11. Bookstore inventory system

3. USE CASE MODEL

A ***use case model*** consists of actors and use cases. It captures services offered by a system and users of the system in terms of actors, use cases, and the *communicate* relationship.

Communicate Relation

The following is a template of a communicate relation (also referred to as an association) between an actor and a single use case. The direction of the arrow indicates the direction of flow of information and direction of interaction. An association could also be outgoing from the use case to the actor to model the response by the system to actors.

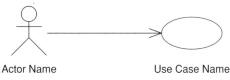

Actor associated with a use case

The relation between a use case and an actor could take several forms: one to one, one to many, or many to many. That is, an actor could be associated with a single use case; in this case, instances of the actor can communicate with the system to get the single service provided by the use case. In a one-to-many relation an actor could communicate with the system to obtain all the services that are captured by the use cases with which the actor is associated. A many-to-many relation permits more than one actor and, consequently, their instances to get the same services from a system.

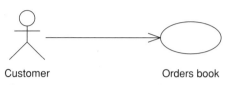

Figure 1-12. **Customer orders books**

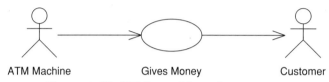

Figure 1-13. ATM machine gives money

Figures 1-12, 1-13, and 1-14 present a few examples of simple association relations, derived from more general use case models, between actors and use cases.

Figure 1-12 is derived from a use case model of a bookstore inventory system. It shows the relationship between the customer actor and the use case *Orders Book*. This use case is the entry point of a real user who wants to use the system to place an order to purchase a book. Similar associations could be depicted between the same actor and other use cases such as *Returns Book*.

Figure 1-13 shows an example, taken from an ATM model, of a use case *Gives Money* associated with two actors, *ATM Machine* and *Customer,* wherein an ATM machine that provides the customer with the money is represented. The *Gives Money* use case captures one of the services that could be provided by the ATM machine to a customer as a result of requesting this service from the machine. In this use case, only the *ATM Machine* actor is active, whereas *Customer* is the passive actor.

Figure 1-14 is an example of a many-to-many relation. Two different actors, *Diskman* and *Walkman,* are associated with two different use cases: *Plays Music* and *Stops Music*.

Figure 1-15 shows a one-to-many association relation. One actor, *Interior Designer,* is associated with three different tasks: *Decorates a House, Sells a Plan,* and *Consults.* Instances of this actor could use three services of the system.

Building a Use Case Model

Building a use case model starts with identifying actors, then use cases of each actor, then relating the two together with the communicate relation. The following is a template of a use case model.

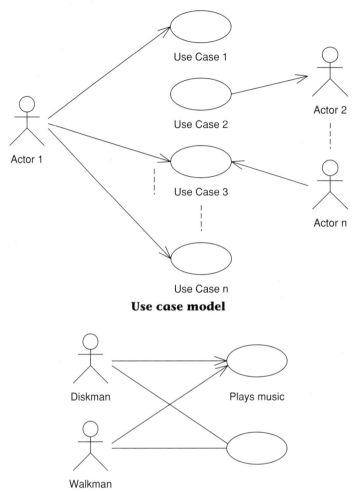

Use case model

Figure 1-14. **Two musical devices playing music**

The importance of a use case model is that it depicts a semiformal model that captures functional requirements of a system in a manner that can be comprehended by real users of the system. Consequently it lays the grounds for making a project case and a project proposal.

Figures 1-16 and 1-17 present a few examples of use case models.

Figure 1-16 shows a simplified use case model with one actor, *Chat User,* of an online chat system. A chat user is an actor that can use the system to add or remove himself from the chat room. The actor can also use the system to send and receive messages when he/she is inside the chat room. The functionality of the system is captured in terms of four different uses of

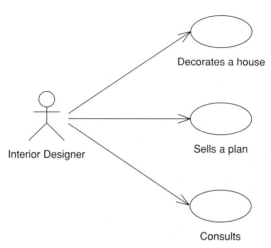

Figure 1-15. The three tasks of an interior designer

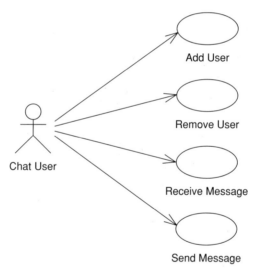

Figure 1-16. Online chat system use case model

the system. The use case *Add User* permits instructing the system to add the user to the chat room. The use case *Remove User* permits instructing the system to remove the user from the chat room. Communication between users in a chat room is modeled with the use cases *Send Message* and *Receive Message*, which permit a user to communicate by sending and receiving messages, respectively.

Figure 1-17 shows a use case model for a software system of a company that is a reseller of goods. The system keeps data on vendors, customers of

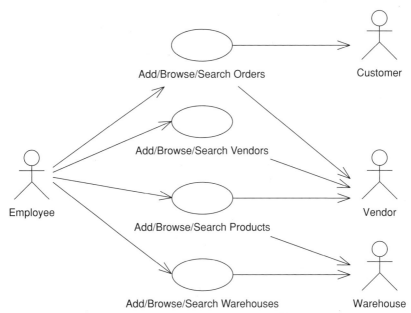

Figure 1-17. **Use case model of a reseller company**

the company, and the warehouses that belong to the company. The model presents four different actors: *Employee, Vendor, Customer,* and *Warehouse.* The first three are active actors that communicate with the system to perform certain functions. *Warehouse* is a passive actor that receives requests via the system as a consequence of requests from the other actors. An *Employee* actor could use the system to manage orders including adding, browsing, or searching for a customer or a vendor; a *Vendor* or *Customer* actor could use the system to browse products in warehouses and to place an order if desired. The various services offered by the system are captured by the use cases *Add/Browse/Search Orders, Add/Browse/Search Vendors, Add/Browse/Search Products,* or *Add/Browse/Search Warehouses.*

Use Case Model with Extends Relationship

Figure 1-18 presents a use case model of a school administration system. The system keeps data on students including biographies of students and academic records. It permits the administration to update data, to produce a printout, and to draw statistical information.

The model presents two main actors: *Secretary* and *Administration.* The administration has the same access rights to the system as that of a secretary, and in addition it can query the system for statistical results. The additional

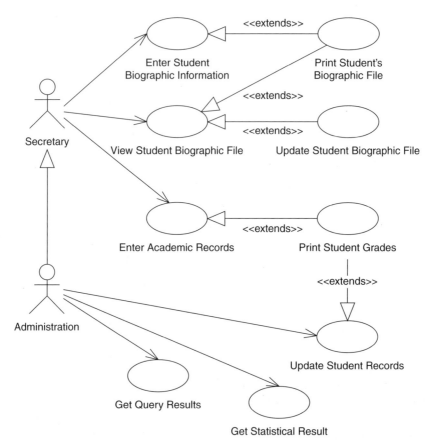

Figure 1-18. School database use case model

access rights are modeled by having the *Administration* actor be a specialization of *Secretary*. The services offered by the system are modeled by a number of use cases. Note the ***extends relationship*** between some of the use cases. In particular, the use case *Update Student Biographic File* extends the use case *View Student Biographic File* because in this case, whenever the *Secretary* wants to update a file, the system implicitly will open the file first. Also, the *Print Student File* use case extends *View Student File,* which implies that the system will open the file first and may permit changes to be made before printing takes place.

Use Case Model with Uses Relationship

Figure 1-19 is a use case model for a computer board game design. This figure illustrates an example of a ***uses relationship*** between use cases. A board

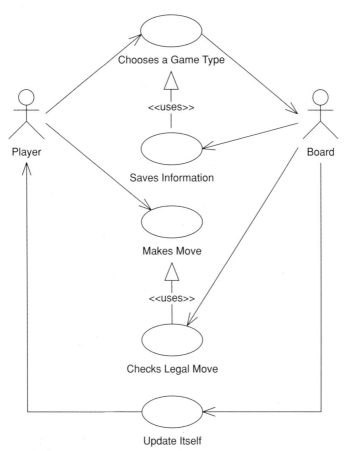

Figure 1-19. **Use case model of a computer game**

game has two actors: *Player* and *Board*. Typical uses that are captured by the use cases include *Chooses the Game Type, Saves Information* on the game, *Makes Move,* and *Update Itself.* The use case *Checks Legal Move* is related to *Makes Move* with the uses relation. *Makes Move* is distinct from *Checks Move,* done by *Board*. However, because it is intended for the *Board* actor to check legality of a move whenever a user makes a move, the two use cases are related by the *uses* relation.

Use Case Model with Interfaces

Use case diagrams can be extended with **interface** notation to model interfaces between actors and use cases. Interfaces capture input that needs to be fed to a use case for the use case to be activated. Interfaces could be between real users and use cases or among software systems, machine networks, telephone lines, and anything from which a use case can receive input.

An interface is modeled as follows.

Interface

Figure 1-20 shows an example of a user interface between the actor *Professor* and the use case *Select Courses to Teach*. The interface is added as an indication that an input such as course name or section number is required to be provided by *Professor* for the use case to be able to offer the required service.

Figure 1-21 shows an example of an output interface between the use case *Return Data* and the *Employee* actor.

Figure 1-22 is a use case diagram with interfaces for a university probation system. The system has three different actors: *Student*, *Responsible*, and *Database*. The actor *Database* keeps data on student records. Using the system, a *Student* actor can query the status of his/her records. *Responsible* models users in charge of managing the system, including updating student records. The model depicts two interfaces: the first is inserted between the *Student* actor and the *GetStatus* use case. This interface is the entry point to the use case that a student user will have to pass through in order to query its status. Such an interface may require a student to enter a password or personal identification for security reasons before entering the database. Another user interface is inserted between actor *Responsible* and the use case *Overview Records*. Again such an interface may be used to provide a secure entry point to the data or simply to provide a user-friendly presentation of the data to the user. Although the model has only three interfaces, other interfaces could be added between actors and use cases and between use cases as well. For example, an interface could be inserted between the use cases *Get Lists* and *GetProbationList* in order to prompt the user to press OK before it continues with refining the main student list to a list of students on probation.

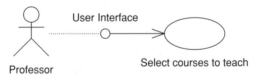

Figure 1-20. User interface

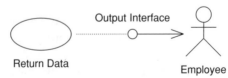

Figure 1-21. Output interface

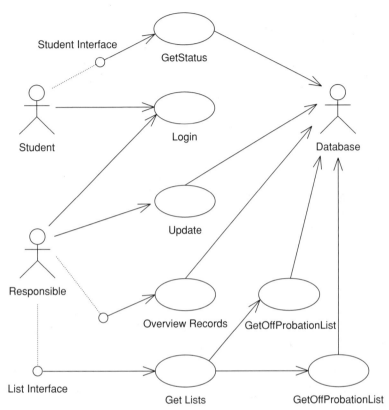

Figure 1-22. **Use case model of a university probation system**

4. PRIMARY SCENARIOS

A ***primary scenario*** describes the flow of activities when a user uses the system based on one of the use cases. A primary scenario is a detailed description of the steps involved in performing a use case and describes sequences of observable behaviors. In doing so, primary scenarios permit a detailed analysis of services of the system without getting involved in details of implementation.

If an activity in a scenario that needs to be performed requires branching on a condition or a repetition, then it is possible to express this behavior in terms of *If* statements to describe conditional situations, or *While* loops to describe repetitions. A primary scenario captures normal behavior, so it excludes exceptions, specific cases, and extensions. These may be expressed using secondary scenarios that are introduced in the forthcoming section.

In terms of a structure, a primary scenario is given a name corresponding to the name of the use case it describes. It starts with a ***precondition*** and concludes with a ***postcondition***. Sequences of behaviors including possible conditionals and loops are inserted between the pre- and postconditions.

A precondition is a condition that must be satisfied in order for a scenario to take place. A postcondition is a condition that when satisfied asserts that a scenario was completed correctly.

We will use the following typical format for describing a primary scenario. The numbers are introduced to assert the order in which the activities will take place upon execution.

- Name of the primary scenario
- Precondition
- Sequence of activities that make the scenario, including branches or repetition; i.e.,
  1. ....
  2. ....
  3. ....
  4. etc.
- Postcondition

Primary scenario

For clarification purposes, Figures 1-23 through 1-26 present primary scenarios for use cases taken from models of various software systems.

Name: Add an officer
Precondition: The officer is not yet registered.
1. The employee enters his password.
2. The employee chooses the "add" option in the menu.
3. The employee fills the required info in the specified places.
4. The employee presses the "submit" button.
5. The officer is added to the system.
Postcondition: The employee logs off.

***Figure 1-23.* Primary scenario of a military officer's organization**

Figure 1-23 is a primary scenario for a use case *AddanOfficer* of a model of a military officer's organization system. *AddanOfficer* permits an employee user to add a new coming officer into the system. The precondition asserts to add an officer, who might not be already registered, to the database. If the precondition is satisfied, the use case will continue with activity number 1 of the scenario. Activities 1 through 5 describe the sequence of interactions between the system and employee necessary to add the new officer to the database. Initially the employee needs to enter his/her password, which confirms his/her eligibility to perform the addition. Next, the add button is chosen from the menu of the system, then data on the new officer is inserted, the submit button is selected, and, finally, the system returns a confirmation that an officer is registered in the system. The postcondition asserts that all the previous steps must have been performed correctly and completely for the employee to be able to log out of the system.

The activities that describe the behavior of a use case may be expressed in a variety of ways – the activities that a system may perform to carry out the use case – depending on the perception of the analyst. This implies that expression of a primary scenario may vary from one analyst to another, which accounts for creativity and subjectivity factors.

Primary Scenario with If Statement

Figure 1-24 gives an example of a primary scenario for use case *Choose a Property* of a real estate software system. The precondition asserts that a user with a valid password or identity logs into the system. The scenario permits two options: view a specific property or browse existing properties before selecting. Note the use of the ***if statement*** to describe branching on these alternatives; either activity 2 or 3 will be performed depending on the satisfaction of the condition expressed by the choice of the user of the system. Activity number 4 ends the use case by having the user select a submit button. The postcondition asserts that the successful termination of the scenario will be followed by logging out of the system or returning to the main menu.

Name: Choose a Property
Precondition: A valid user has logged into the system.
1. The use case starts when the customer chooses to buy a property.
2. If the customer chooses to view all the available properties
   a) the system displays all the offers available.
   b) the customer chooses among the offers.
3. If the customer chooses to view a specific property
   a) the customer has to fill in a property information form.
   b) the customer enters the house type, the area, and the budget.
4. The use case finishes when the customer selects Submit.
Alternative path: The buyer can select cancel at any time.
Postcondition: The system returns home or exits completely.

Figure 1-24. Primary scenario of a real estate system

Figure 1-25 is another primary scenario for the *Retrieve* use case of a military officer's organization. The primary scenario describes the activities required so that an *Employee* can retrieve information about a specific officer.

Name: Retrieve Officer's Information
Precondition: The employee logs in.
1. The employee chooses the option "search."
2. The employee enters the ID of the officer.
3. The employee presses the "submit" button.
4. If the officer's data is available
    The information is displayed.
5. Else if data are not available
    a) The system returns a warning message.
    b) The system asks the employee to get the information.
Postcondition: The employee logs out.

Figure 1-25. Primary scenario of a retrieve use case of military officer's organization

A primary scenario can always rely on if-like statements to express branching. Figures 1-24 and 1-25 rely on if statements to capture two alternatives only. However, a scenario could use if then else with several else alternatives, if necessary.

Primary Scenario with While Loop Statement

A primary scenario may also express repetition of one or more activities. A while loop could be used to capture such repetition.

Figure 1-26 is a primary scenario with repetition of use case *Overview Record* of the university probation system. The precondition states that the login ID and password of *Responsible* in charge need to be accepted by the system in order for the remaining activities to continue. After logging in, *Responsible* may repeatedly query the system to retrieve information on specific students. The repetition is expressed in activity number 4 using the ***while loop statement***.

A primary scenario may use more than one loop. It may also use nested while or if statements, or a combination of these in any manner that permits the expression of activities of a primary scenario.

5. SECONDARY SCENARIOS

A ***secondary scenario*** describes instances and special situations, such as alternatives or problems that occur in certain rare and unexpected situations.

Name: Overview Record
Precondition: The login and password of the responsible are valid.
1. The responsible selects Overview Record from the Main Menu.
2. The system queries the database.
3. The system outputs a list of all the students who were once put on probation and the dates when they were placed or removed if this case applies.
4. While the responsible selects a student ID from the list and presses the Find key.
   a) The system queries the database.
   b) The system outputs detailed information about this student such as the number of semesters he was placed on probation.
   c) The responsible presses close.
   d) The system goes back to the list.
5. The system goes back to the Main Menu.
Postcondition: The system is back to the Main Menu.

***Figure 1-26.* Primary scenario of a university probation system**

An ***alternative scenario*** is used for expressing sequences of events that modify a primary scenario to capture an exception and unexpected behaviors. A secondary scenario may also capture nonfunctional requirements such as time of response and returning conditions.

We will use the following typical format for describing a secondary scenario. It may be presented independently, as in the template, or it may be added at the end of the primary scenario with which it is associated.

- Name of the secondary scenario
- Primary scenario name to which it refers
- Description of the problem or alternative faced

Secondary scenario

Figures 1-27, 1-28, 1-29, and 1-30 give examples of secondary scenarios.

Figure 1-27 is a secondary scenario of the "Add an Officer" primary scenario of the military officer's organization system already described in Figure 1-23. The scenario emits a message when an invalid password is entered by the user.

> **Name:** Invalid password
> **Primary Scenario:** Add an Officer
> The employee typed a wrong password.

Figure 1-27. "Invalid password" secondary scenario

Figure 1-28 is a secondary scenario of the "Choose a Property" primary scenario for the real state software already described in Figure 2-24. The scenario warns the user that the entered data are incomplete.

> **Name:** Missing data
> **Primary Scenario:** Choose a Property
> The type of housing, the regional requirement, and the budget are not specified.

Figure 1-28. "Missing data" secondary scenario

Figure 1-29 is a secondary scenario of the primary scenario of Figure 1-25, "Retrieve Officer's Information." The scenario puts a condition on response time. If the database does not respond in a certain time limit with requested information then a time-out error message would be emitted.

> **Name:** Time Response Error
> **Primary Scenario:** Retrieve Officer's Information
> The database holds a large amount of data, which might take a lot of time for the execution of the query and can result in a time response error.

Figure 1-29. "Time response error" secondary scenario

Another example of a secondary scenario of the primary scenario of Figure 1-26 is shown in Figure 1-30. Here the system could return an error message and terminate the search session if details of a nonregistered student are entered.

> **Name:** Not Registered
> **Primary Scenario:** Overview Records
> The student is not registered for the current semester and the responsible is trying to retrieve his current status.

Figure 1-30. "Not registered" secondary scenario

A primary scenario may have more than one secondary scenario, each of which expresses a condition. Secondary scenarios help to account for possible atypical activities of use cases.

6. ACTIVITY DIAGRAM

An **activity diagram** is a state transition diagram that consists of **states** and **transitions** between states. It is a graphical representation of a scenario and its constituent activities. A state captures a snapshot of the system during execution. A transition captures the transition of the system from one state to another brought about by performing an activity.

The following is a template for the notation of a state. A state is modeled using a rounded-corner rectangle. Each state is given a name that denotes the current activity of the system captured by the state.

State Name

State

An activity diagram has a single **start state** and one or more **end states**. The start state is modeled by a black circle, whereas the end state is modeled by a bull's-eye. Arrows model transition from one state to another. The following are templates for the notation for a start state and an end state.

●   ◉

Start state   **End state**

In what follows we present a few examples of activity diagrams that correspond to models and scenarios introduced earlier in the chapter.

Figure 1-31 shows an activity diagram for a chat user using an online chat system for sending messages. The diagram consists of three states and two transitions. The activity starts with the user logging into the system, sending a message, and logging out.

Figure 1-31. Activity diagram for a single send session of an online chat system

Branching

Because activity diagrams capture semantics of scenarios graphically, these could capture conditionals and repetition, as well as secondary scenarios.

Activity diagrams can capture **branching** from one state using two different transitions. Iteration may be modeled by a transition from the state to itself.

Figure 1-32 shows a more detailed version of the activity diagram in Figure 1-31. It depicts send and receive sessions. The activity diagram has four states other than the start and end states: *Login, Send, Receive,* and *Logout.* After logging into a system, a user may choose to engage in a send or receive session. Once a send or receive occurs the system makes a transition to one of the corresponding states *Send* or *Receive,* where a user could repeatedly engage in send or receive sessions or alternate between the two (note the transition from state *Send* (and *Receive*) to itself). From either state a user can choose to log out of the system. The activity terminates when the user logs out of the system.

Constraints

Some transitions may be subject to **constraints**. A constraint is a condition that needs to be satisfied for a transition from a state to occur. Constraints may be represented between square brackets and be tagged to transitions.

Figure 1-33 shows an activity diagram for a general password-based transaction. The activity diagram has four states: *Reading, Validating, Displaying Message,* and *Performing Transaction.* The *Reading* state is the initial state in which the input is read. *Validating* is the state in which the legality of the password is validated. State *Reading* terminates and a transition to state

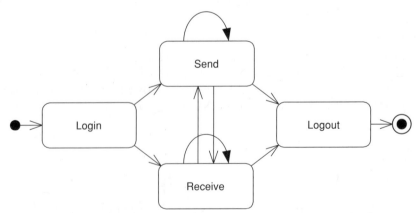

Figure 1-32. Activity diagram for a complete chat session

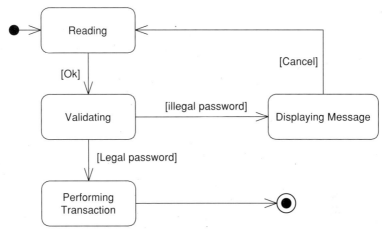

Figure 1-33. Activity diagram for a password-based transaction

Validating occurs when the *[OK]* constraint is satisfied. The *[Illegal Password]* constraint shows that activity would change from the *Validating* state to the *Displaying Message* state if the password is illegal; otherwise, the system moves into the *Performing Transaction* state where requested transactions could be performed.

Looping

Loops may be modeled by transitions, using backward arrows from a state to a previous state and from a state to itself as in Figure 1-32.

Figure 1-34 shows an activity diagram for the use case *Delete Biographical Student Information* of a student information system.

The activity has six different states. The constraints on the transitions capture conditions that need to be satisfied for a transition to occur. Note the loops captured with the back arrows from the states *Information not Deleted* and *Specified Information Deleted* to state *Delete Form Displayed*. The loops generated by these transitions permit a user of the system to repeatedly delete any number of forms as may be required. This activity has two end states, meaning that the activity may terminate in either of the end states depending on the choice of a user of the system.

Simultaneous States

A template representing two states starting to ***work simultaneously*** is given as follows.

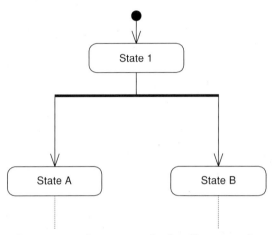

States starting to work simultaneously

After the completion of state 1, the two states A and B start to perform a simultaneous job. This could be used to model a system with parallel processes.

Figure 1-35 shows an activity diagram that captures state and transitions that a person performs in the process of watching television. Note that when

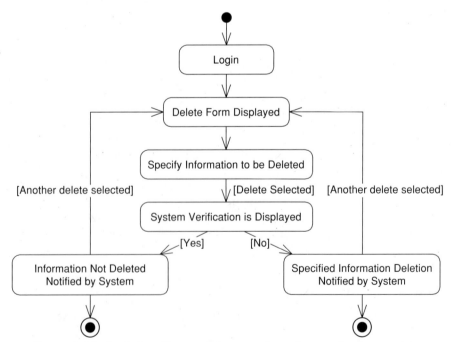

Figure 1-34. Activity diagram for a university probation system

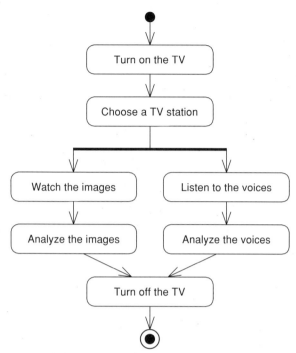

***Figure 1-35.* Activity diagram for a person watching television**

a station is selected, two activities proceed simultaneously until the television is turned off. The first activity is captured by the states *Watch the Images* and *Analyze the Images* and the intermediate transition. The other activity focuses on voices.

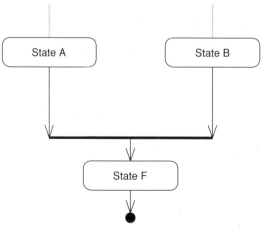

States finishing simultaneously

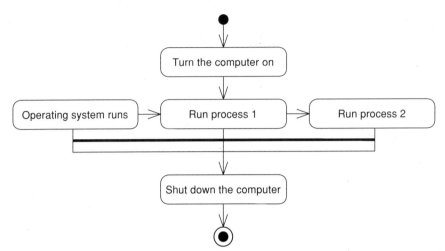

***Figure 1-36.* Activity diagram for a computer system**

The preceding template is another template representing two states *fin-ishing simultaneously*.

Figure 1-36 is the activity diagram representing states that a computer passes through from turning it on until shutting it down. All processes terminate simultaneously when a computer is turned off.

7. OBJECTS AND CLASSES

Objects are run-time abstractions that communicate at run time by message passing to perform an activity. Objects could abstract behavior of a variety of real objects such as system users, boundary systems, objects such as bikes, computers, animals, radios, commands, and any object whose activity affects the system's behavior.

A ***class*** is a programming abstraction that captures statically the behavior of objects. A class describes the state of objects in terms of attributes (data members) and behavior in terms of methods (functions and procedures). An ***attribute*** captures a possible state of an object, whereas a ***method*** (also known as an operation) implements an activity or service of the object. Objects are the dynamic counterpart of classes. An object is created at run time as an instance of a class abstraction. Several objects may be created as instances of a single class. ***Objects*** are dynamic entities in the sense that they are created and exist at run time as instances of classes. Also, attribute values may be updated at run time as a result of method execution. Objects are purely dynamic, in the sense that they are destroyed at run time. Alternatively, objects could be persistent between runs of the same program, such as database objects used to keep persistent data.

The following is the UML template of a class.

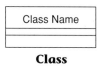

Class

Figure 1-37 shows examples of classes of software systems for a rent-a-car company. Note the class *Car*. Although there is one class car, the system would account for an unlimited number of car objects that differ in terms of color, model, make, and other attributes. Similarly, there is one class *Client* but the system could handle data on an unlimited number of clients. Each client of the real clients would be a *client object* that is an instance of class *Client*.

Figure 1-38 shows examples of classes of a software system for the library. *Journal* and *Archive* are examples of persistent objects that keep data that must persist between runs of the library system. Class *Librarian* abstracts the activity of a librarian that manages the system. The data of a specific librarian need not persist, like in the case of *Journal*, so librarian objects are created and destroyed at run time.

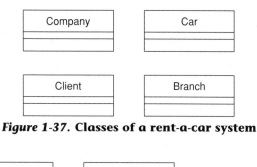

Figure 1-37. Classes of a rent-a-car system

Figure 1-38. Classes of a library system

Classes with Attributes

Attributes are the data fields of classes that abstract the data that objects need to keep. A class would include as attributes data fields that abstract commonalities among objects. At run time the values of these attributes would vary from one object to another.

Figure 1-39 shows classes *Book* and *Librarian* with attributes. Class *Book* has three attributes: name, ISBN, and date of production (DOP). String, Integer, and Date are types of the attributes; Integer is a basic type, whereas Date and String are class types, that is, these stand for class names that contain data and operations. The three attributes of class *Book* indicate that any book object needs to keep a string to stand for its name, an ISBN, and DOP. These attributes vary from one object to another because different book objects would have different names, ISBNs, and DOP. Similarly the *Librarian* class keeps two attributes: name and ID. All librarians have names and IDs but distinct librarian objects would have different names and IDs.

Attributes carry types that could be basic values such as integer and real or that could be class names. For example, a class *Book* could have an attribute author name: Author where Author is defined as a class abstraction that carries the author's name, address, and list of publications.

***Figure 1-39.* Book and Librarian classes with attributes**

Classes with Operations

Operations are methods that abstract services of objects. Services may be exported, allowing other objects to invoke these or internal services to be used by other methods and operations of the same objects. All objects that are instances of the same class have the same operations.

Figure 1-40 shows classes *Book* and *Librarian* with operations. Class *Book* has two operations: *borrow( )* and *return( )*. *Borrow( )* is the activity that is invoked upon a request to borrow a book object. *Return( )* is the activity that is invoked when a borrowed object is to be returned. Similarly, the *Librarian* class has a single operation *register( )* that is the same for all *Librarian* objects.

Some operations may need input to perform the activity. In this case operations could be given parameters. For instance, if the *register( )* operation of class librarian requires a date, then it would have been introduced instead as *register(d: Date)*. Similarly, if operation *borrow( )* of class *Book* requires the name and ID of the borrower then it would have been introduced as *borrow (name: String, id: Integer)* where name and id are parameters whose actual value would vary with the name and ID of the borrower.

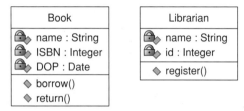

Figure 1-40. **Book and Librarian classes with operations**

Parameterized Class

Classes may be ***parameterized*** over a type when it is possible for the class abstraction to hold the same attribute and carry the same operations for different types of attributes or operation parameters. The following is the general template of a parameterized class. *P* denotes the parameter.

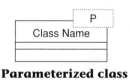

Parameterized class

Figure 1-41 is an example of a list that can hold any type of objects, such as books, journals, general publications, strings, and integers, to mention a few. Hence, instead of defining a class abstraction for each type, one parameterized class abstraction is defined. The parameter *P* is used in the class abstraction to introduce declaration like any other type. For example, the class list could have an operation *sort(lst: P)* that sorts a list *lst*. The parameter *P* is associated

Figure 1-41. **Parameterized List class**

with the actual type in declarations of attributes and method parameters. For example, a class *Company* could have a list of employees declared as *employees: List[Employee]*, where *Employee* is the class abstraction that holds attributes and operations on employees. Similarly, a library could have a list of journals and books. Then two attributes would be introduced: *books: List[book]* and *journals: List[journal]*. In all of the previous three examples, the actual class names, *Employee, Book,* and *Journal,* would replace the parameter *P* of Class *List* anywhere that *P* appears in a declaration in class *List*, particularly in the declaration of the parameter of operation *sort(lst: P)*.

Associations

Classes may be related by client–supplier relationship. An **association** models such a relation between a client and a supplier. The association reads a one-to-one relation for each instance of the client class that there is a corresponding instance of a supplier class. Alternatively, associations may be tagged with multiplicity notations that model the number of supplier objects that may be created to correspond to one or many clients.

One-to-one Association

Figure 1-42 shows an example of **one-to-one association**.

The verb phrase "manages" on the link describes the association. Any company has a single general manager who manages it. The notation 1 means "one and only one." The association reads: "A General Manager manages A Company."

One-to-many Association

Figure 1-43 shows an example of a **one-to-many association**. The verb phrase on the link describes the association. In the company car example, the *Company* class is the client of the *Car* class. The notation 0..* means "zero or many." The association reads: "A Company owns many Cars."

Figure 1-42. One-to-one association

Figure 1-43. One-to-many association

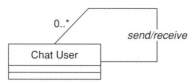

Figure 1-44. Self-association in a chat system

Self Association

A class may be related to itself as follows.

The association in Figure 1-44 reads: "A chat User may send and receive messages to and from Chat Users." Note that class *Chat User* captures the behavior of all users. Dynamically different instances of *Chat User* would be created and those would engage in send and receive sessions.

Many-to-many Association

Figure 1-45 shows associations among three classes. The association between *Reservation* and *Flights* is many to many because a reservation system can display information on many flights and flights' information can appear on many reservation systems. An *Agent* can access many reservation systems to display information, make a reservation, or get any other reservation service.

Aggregation

An ***aggregation*** is a relation between classes that models "consist of" relations. Aggregations may be viewed as special kinds of associations. Like associations, aggregations may be tagged with multiplicity notation.

A template of one example of an ***aggregation association*** is shown as follows. *X* and *Y* denote two class abstractions. The diamond denotes the aggregation relation. Such a template reads as follows: "*X* consists of *Y*." It is possible for one class to be related by aggregation to more than one class, as shall be demonstrated in some of the following examples.

Aggregation

Figure 1-46 shows how a relation between a company that consists of one or more branches may be modeled. The notation 1..* means "one or many." The association reads: "The Company consists of one or many Branches."

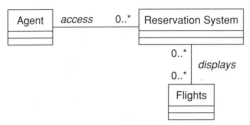

Figure 1-45. Many-to-many association in a reservation system

Figure 1-46. Company consists of one-to-many branches

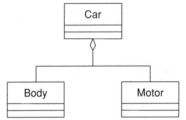

Figure 1-47. Aggregation among several classes

Figure 1-47 shows how aggregation may be used to model the consist relation between a class and several constituent classes. The model reads: "A Car consists of a Body and a Motor."

Generalization

A *generalization* relation models an "is-a" relation between two classes or one parent and several children classes. Class *A* is a generalization of another class *B* if we can express the following: *B* is an *A*. For example, a class *Computing Machine* could be related to another class *Computer* via a generalization relation. We say that a *Computing Machine* is a generalization of class *Computer*.

Another name for generalization is inheritance or parent–descendant relation. For example, the generalization concept among classes is similar to the generalization concept between actors introduced earlier. Generalization is a one-way relation and it is transitive. That is, if *A* is a generalization of another class *B* then *B* could not be a generalization of *A*. In such a case *A* would be the parent class, and *B* the descendant. Transitivity means that if a class *A* is a generalization of another class *B* and *B* is a generalization of a third class *C*, then *A* is a generalization of class *C*.

A template of the generalization association is as follows.

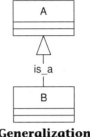

Generalization

Two classes may be related by inheritance to serve several objectives. Some of these are

- Sharing: *B* would inherit *A* to permit class *B* to share attributes and operations of class *A*

- Specialization: *B* would inherit *A* to acquire and then specialize some of the behaviors of class *A*

- Combination: *B* would inherit more than one class to combine features of these classes into one class abstraction

- Implementation: *B* would inherit features of a generic class to make these features more adaptable in a specific context.

Figures 1-48 to 1-50 include subsystem model examples on generalization relation.

Figure 1-48 shows an excerpt of a model for a software company. Class *Client* is a generalization of class *Employee*. Class *Employee* inherits class *Client* to permit an employee to have the same access privileges as a client. Note that every employee could be a client of the company but not every client is an employee.

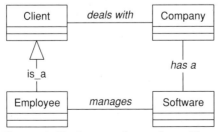

Figure 1-48. **An employee is a client**

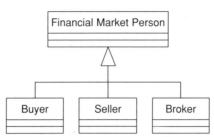

Figure 1-49. Buyer, Seller, and Broker are Financial Market Persons

Figure 1-49 shows how generalization may be used to model an is-a relation between a class and several constituent classes. This figure refers to the
different types of persons who work in the financial market field. An example
of this could be a buyer of a call/put option, a seller of a call/put option, and
the broker who works as an intermediary. Each buyer, seller, and broker is a
financial market person. This is expressed by making classes *Buyer, Seller,* and
Broker inherit the more general class *Financial Market Person.*

The last two examples (Figures 1-50 and 1-51) in this section present
somewhat more developed models of a school database and joke-teller
system that account for all the concepts introduced earlier in single
framework.

Figure 1-50 is a detailed example of an object model for a school database.
The school database allows the user to manipulate different options, such
as providing a student with financial aid, retrieving data about the student
family, and assigning courses to a student. Note how the aggregation relation is used here. We have the student who belongs to a family that consists of a mother, a father, and siblings (brothers and sisters). Also note
how the inheritance relationship is used to have secretary, social worker,
and accounting team all acquire user behavior by inheriting from the class
User.

Figure 1-51 represents an object model for joke-teller software. The joke-
teller software has the purpose of entertaining its users with jokes. A user can
add a joke to an existing database on jokes, read existing jokes, and search for
a certain joke. In order to access the system the user has to provide a password
that permits the system to identify him/her uniquely. The object model has
four classes: *Joke, Comment, User,* and *Password.* Class *Joke* models the interface to a database on jokes and permits modification of the database. Class
User models user objects. Class *Comment* permits a user to attach a comment,
such as good, bad, or funny, to a joke; note that a joke can be given many
comments. The operations listed in the classes summarize the functionality
of each class.

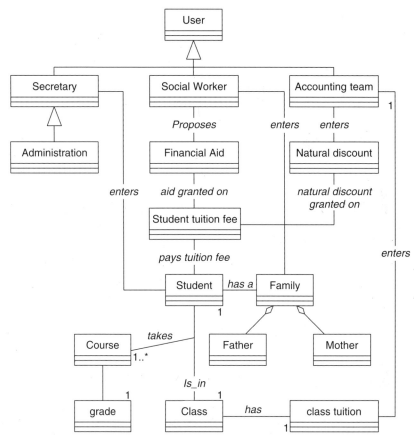

Figure 1-50. Object model of a school database

8. SEQUENCE AND COLLABORATION DIAGRAMS

Sequence Diagrams

A ***sequence diagram*** shows object interactions arranged in a time sequence. It depicts the objects and classes involved in a scenario and the sequence of messages exchanged between the objects needed to carry out the functionality of the scenario.

- They are modeled in terms of classes and lifelines.

- Single-headed arrows $\longrightarrow$ model message passing at some time during the life of an object.

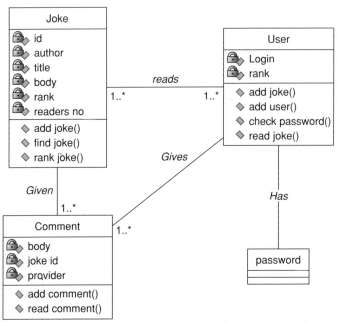

***Figure 1-51.* Joke-teller object model**

- Condition may be associated with message passing:

  [Condition] message name (method call) →

- A * before a message name indicates iteration; that is, the message will be sent repeatedly.

- The following models a message from an object to itself:

- The following models a return situation: ⟵

In general, message returns are not included for simplicity. It is better to include them when you consider that they are necessary to clarify communication between objects.

Sequence diagrams can be derived from scenarios that describe communication between objects of the class diagram model.

To derive a sequence diagram:

1. Describe a scenario of interaction between two or more objects.

2. Draw a lifeline for each object.

3. For each request from an object A to an object B, model it with an outgoing arrow.

4. If a message return is essential for another message to proceed, then the return must be modeled explicitly with the arrow ⟶ or replaced with a condition on the message that depends on it. Figures 2-52 and 2-53 show generalized sequence diagrams.

5. Model iteration as described earlier.

Figure 1-52 represents a sequence diagram where message m2 cannot proceed before r1 is done; hence, it models the situation where message m2 depends on r1. Another way of representing this dependence is represented in Figure 1-53 where, instead of having three arrows between the two objects 1 and 2, we have two arrows with a condition on the second arrow.

Figure 1-54 represents a sequence diagram for a bookstore inventory system. This sequence diagram represents the total process of ordering a book in a bookstore. It has three objects: the customer, the bookstore, and the book. The customer orders a requested book from the bookstore. The bookstore responsible locates it in the books database. If the book is found, the price is returned to the customer, who will pay for it and get the book from the bookstore.

In buying a property application, the system will display the buying agreement to the customer. The customer will give his credit card number that a specialized system *Money Handling* will validate. Then the system will store

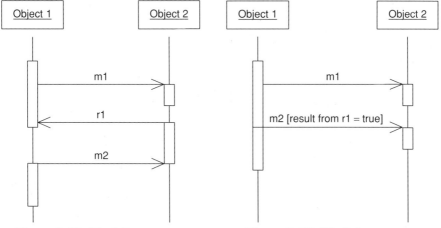

***Figure 1-52.* Model sequence diagram**   ***Figure 1-53.* Model sequence diagram**

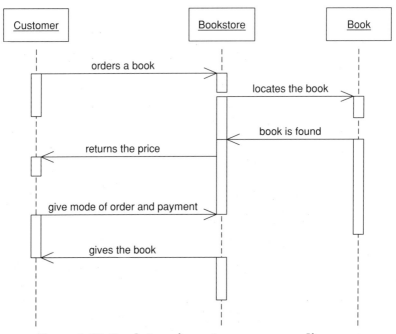

Figure 1-54. Bookstore inventory sequence diagram

the customer information in its database, add him/her as a new customer, and provide the customer with a new property.

The sequence diagram of buying a property is represented in Figure 1-55.

We have four objects: *Customer*, *System*, *Database*, and *Money Handling*. Whenever the customer wants to buy a property, he/she has to accept the agreement conditions displayed by the system. Then, he/she has to submit his/her credit card number to the money handling subsystem. In case the number is false, he/she has to resubmit the information again until the credit card number is a valid one. After this, the system will retrieve the customer information from the database, update the information, and mark the property chosen by the customer as sold. Finally, the customer has bought the property.

Collaboration Diagrams

A *collaboration diagram* models interaction among objects. The order in which messages are passed is indicated with a number. Collaboration diagrams model interaction and conditional cases better than sequence diagrams.

Collaboration diagrams differ from sequence diagrams in that they capture ordered sequencing, but without including separate life lines like in sequence

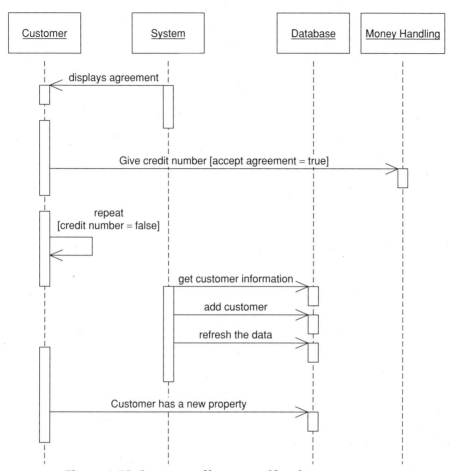

Figure 1-55. Sequence diagram of buying a property

diagrams. In fact, by having the sequence diagram, it is quite easy to come up with the collaboration diagram and vice versa.

The collaboration diagram for the sequence diagram in Figure 1-54 is given in Figure 1-56.

The numbers are there to indicate the correct step sequence occurring in the corresponding scenario. The arrows model the direction of the action being undertaken in each step of the diagram. For example, the first step is "orders a book" and it is directed from the object *Customer* to the object *Bookstore*.

Another example appears in Figure 1-57, which represents an ATM system.

As we see, the user has to insert his card into the ATM machine. The ATM machine has then to go through a long process in interaction with consortium

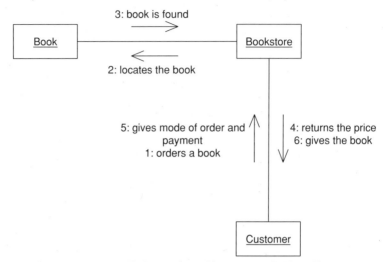

Figure 1-56. Collaboration diagram of a bookstore

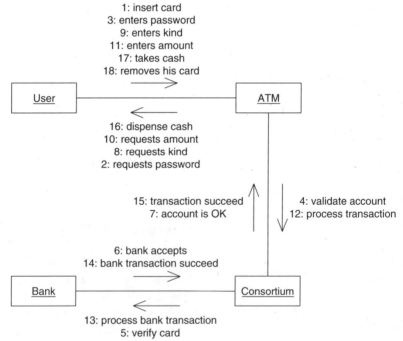

Figure 1-57. Collaboration diagram of an ATM system

and bank objects in order to validate the card. Then the user will be able to retrieve the amount of money needed from the ATM.

9. SYSTEM ARCHITECTURE

The **architecture** of a system captures the following:

- The organization of the system in terms of subsystems that compose the target software systems. A **subsystem** is the collection of classes of a system that collectively captures one behavior of the main system.

- The model of communication among subsystems including direction of flow of data among the systems.

- Interfaces that constitute external services offered by the system or channels by which a system can communicate with external agents.

In determining the architecture of a system, three answers need to be provided for three key questions:

- What are the subsystems? Leading to the subsystems.

- How do these communicate? Leading to the communication model.

- What do these communicate? Leading to interfaces that include services and data that could be communicated.

A good architecture is one wherein subsystems have strong cohesion; that is, the objects of which they are composed have strong functional relationships in terms of the services they provide to other subsystems. The subsystems need to be loosely coupled; that is, they should have as few interactions as possible.

Communication-wise, subsystems relate by *peer-to-peer* relation, where data can be communicated in both directions between the systems, and by *client–supplier* relation, where the client module can use services of the supplier, and not vice versa.

Figure 1-58 shows the architecture for any ordering site in the web where the customer accesses the site and makes an order.

Manage Order will handle the orders entered by the customer in the site. Also, the *Manage Order* subsystem has an interface to the database, which it will use to check and update the database. The site order subsystem allows the customer to view information, fill an order form, or cancel an order form.

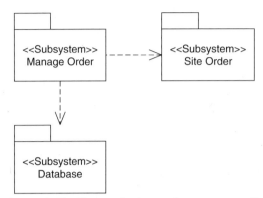

Figure 1-58. Site ordering subsystem model

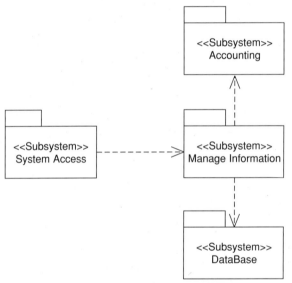

Figure 1-59. Consulting company subsystem model

The subsystem *Manage Order* will get the customer order information from the *Site Order* subsystem. Then it will go to the database and check for the availability of the goods ordered, update the content of the database, and process the order.

Figure 1-59 shows another example of a subsystem model for a consulting company.

This subsystem model is a typical model for any management consulting company. *System Access* is necessary to handle the security part of the system. The *Manage Information* subsystem is responsible for managing the data entered by the user. The result is then sent to the database subsystem, where it will be stored, and to the accounting subsystem, where the cost and revenue will be calculated for every new project.

10. CONCLUSION

This chapter introduced artifacts used to capture analysis, design, and implementation of object-oriented software models. The chapter focused on artifacts that the *bridge* process uses in capturing software models.

Chapter 2

Bridge: A Systematic Process Model

*This chapter introduces the general process model on which the developed case studies were based. It commences with an overview of software development phases and general process models as a preamble to introducing the **bridge** process model based on which the case studies in the forthcoming chapters were developed.*

1. AN OVERVIEW OF PROCESS MODELS

Several process models were discussed and developed to provide a set of activities that permits the development of software systems from user requirements. Almost all processes follow the development of software through the following phases: analysis, design, and implementation, in addition to system testing.

Analysis is the phase during which user requirements are determined and requirement specifications are documented. User requirements are typically collected in a language that is familiar to the user, where a user in this context could mean a real user, the company, or a vendor that requests the software to be developed to automate certain services. The *requirements* describe **what** the system is requested to deliver as automated services. Requirements are documented in a specification language that is understood by the designers and developers and that steps away from the user, creating, more or less, a gap between the language and requirements expressed by the user and language and tools applied by analysts, designers, and implementers. The output of this phase is a requirement specification document.

The *design* phase follows analysis. During design a system designer relies on system specifications reached during the analysis phase to lay out the design of the system. The design captures *how* the system will implement the specifications. System designs are expressed in a variety of artifacts. In an object-oriented approach, classes and objects as well as components may be used to express the design of a system.

Implementation is the phase during which code is introduced in a specific programming language and paradigm.

Testing is the process that includes verification and validation. Validation is the process during which the resulting implemented system is checked against user requirements. A system is valid if it delivers the services that were requested by the user. Verification is the process during which a system is tested to ensure that it is free of errors. Note that it is only possible to ensure that a system is free of the error that it was tested for. Although it may be possible to verify that a system is free of certain errors, the same system may be considered invalid when it does not satisfy user requirements.

The aforementioned phases have been incorporated into several models of software development. The main two approaches are the discrete and iterative approaches. In a discrete approach, the development of a system can move from one phase into another in the order in which they were presented – that is, analysis, design, implementation, and testing – when the previous phase is concluded. The waterfall model follows this approach. The iterative approach is incremental in nature. In this category the development of the system iterates among the described phases. For instance, design could start directly during analysis. Also, code could be introduced with the design artifacts. Models based on object-oriented concepts follow this approach. Classes are sometimes used as analysis and design expression artifacts in addition to being the main programming abstractions.

The unified software development process models development as incremental phases of iterative cycles. Each phase includes four subphases: inception, elaboration, construction, and transition. The analysis, design, implementation, and testing activities are integrated into the subphases so that each concludes with a product release. Inception is the main phase during which analysis is performed. A skeleton of the system is produced during the elaboration phase. Construction is the phase wherein the system is implemented.

In general, models with discrete approaches prove to be suitable to managers who need a norm to rely on when measuring project progress. Iterative models serve to minimize gaps between deliverables and are prone to adaptation to satisfy user requirements during any of the phases. This advantage helps to balance the disadvantage of the indiscrete and undefined nature of the iteration involved.

2. AN OVERVIEW OF THE BRIDGE PROCESS

The **Bridge** process integrates traditional phases of software development – design, analysis, and implementation – and phases of the unified software development approach – inception, elaboration, and construction. The objective of bridge is to rationalize the development process and elaborate it in a systematic stepwise refinement manner with the objective of reaching a valid system via a sequence of iterative yet predetermined tasks beginning with user requirements on through to product delivery.

Bridge comprises four main development activities: analysis, design, implementation, and testing. In addition it has three main phases, the inception, elaboration, and construction phases. Each of the phases includes the four activities to varying degrees. Bridge specifies the number of iterations and deliverables of each iteration within each phase, as the result of each activity is specified. Also the tactic of producing each deliverable is also described.

Because of its rigor, bridge caters to loopholes in iterative processes, increasing the potential of reaching software system validity systematically. First, by specifying a language-based approach for obtaining deliverables, it permits rationalization of the development process without eliminating the ingenuity of the developer. Second, by specifying the number of iterations, it eliminates the uncertainty factor introduced by iterative approaches. Third, by specifying deliverables of each activity and discrete cuts among the phases, it allows for benefits of iteration to endure with the benefits of the norm of discreteness. Fourth, the bridge process is accompanied by a traceability model that guides the developer in establishing traces systematically from user requirements to implementation artifacts yet gives assurances to the validity of the software under development at specific points throughout the development cycle.

Figure 2-1 gives a snapshot of phases, activities, and iterations of the bridge process. The inception phase consists mainly of capturing user requirements with a use case model. The elaboration phase is mostly analysis with a preliminary design; it focuses on detailing the use case model. Several versions of the use case model may be derived. In addition, an initial object model is produced and the system is divided into subsystems. The design starts with deciding on the main subsystems. The construction phase is divided into two

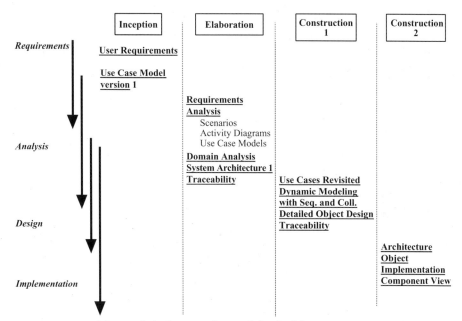

Figure 2-1. **A snapshot of the bridge process**

subphases. Subphase 1 is mostly design with preliminary implementation; subphase 2 is mostly implementation.

Figure 2-2 gives a linear view of the bridge process. It clearly shows how iteration is linearized and discretized to result in specific deliverables for each activity within a phase. The bridge process relies on the following artifacts for capturing deliverables:

- *Use Case Model* for capturing requirements specification.

- *Object Model* and its constituents, including classes, objects, and associations, for capturing design.

- *Components* and related relationship for capturing *Architecture.*

- *Scenarios, Activity Diagrams,* and *State Diagrams* for refinement and bridging purposes.

It is clear that the number of required iterations is specified. In particular the use case model undergoes four iterations. The first iteration in the inception phase results in a specification of the functionality of the system. Two following refinements are reached in the elaboration phases based on scenarios and activity diagrams. The fourth and final iteration is reached at the

1. Inception

1.1 Determining User Requirements
1.2 Determining Use Case Model
 1.2.1 Identification of Actors
 1.2.2 Identification of Use Cases
 1.2.3 Use Case Model (version 1)
1.3 Giving a Glossary

2. Elaboration

2.1 Requirements Analysis (refining the use case model)
 2.1.1 Primary Scenarios
 2.1.2 Use Case Model Version 2
 2.1.3 Activity Diagrams
 2.1.4 Secondary Scenarios
 2.1.5 Use Case Diagrams Version 3
2.2 Domain Analysis (deriving an initial object model)
 2.2.1 Determining Objects
 2.2.2 Determining Associations
 2.2.3 Determining Attributes
2.3 Subsystem Analysis
2.4 Traceability
 2.4.1 Use Cases to Objects
 2.4.2 Objects to Architecture

3. Construction/Design (phase 1)

3.1 Use Cases Revisited (Use Case Model Version 4)
3.2 Dynamic Modeling (includes sequence and collaboration diagrams)
3.3 Detailed Object Design (Object Model Version 2)
3.4 Traceability
 3.4.1 Use Cases to Objects
 3.4.2 Objects to Architecture (details the architecture)

4. Construction/Implementation (phase 2)

4.1 Implementation Language and Environment
4.2 Physical Architecture
4.3 Object Implementation (Object Model Version 3)
 4.3.1 State Diagrams
 4.3.2 Class Implementation
 4.3.3 New Classes
4.4 Component View

5. Construction/Testing

5.1 Verification
5.2 Validation

Figure 2-2. **A linear view of the bridge process model**

Phase	Deliverable
Inception	User Requirements
	Actors
	Use Cases
	Use Case Model Version 1
Elaboration	Primary Scenarios
	Activity Diagrams
	Use Case Model Version 2
	Secondary Scenarios
	Use Case Model Version 3
	Objects
	Associations
	Initial Object Model
	Initial Subsystem's Model
	Trace
Construction 1	**Use Cases Model Version 4**
	Sequence Diagrams
	Collaboration Diagrams
	Object Model Version 2
	Subsystem's Model Version 2
	Trace 2

Figure 2-3. **Deliverables of the bridge process**

beginning of the construction phase. The object model undergoes three iterations. The first object model is derived in the elaboration phase, the second in the first part of the construction phase, and the last, with full-fledged implementation, in the second part of construction. Traceability is repeated at least twice: at the end of the elaboration and at the first part of the construction phase.

Figure 2-3 summarizes the deliverables of bridge at different phases in the temporal order in which they are produced. Only deliverables of the first part of the construction phase are introduced. The main deliverable of the second part of the construction phase is the final implementation. Note that the key deliverables for traceability and validation purposes are highlighted.

Because bridge mainly concerns the analysis and design phases, the construction phase is divided into two phases. The second phase is excluded from Figure 2-3 because it mainly concerns implementation.

3. INCEPTION PHASE

The **inception** phase is the phase where user requirements are determined, and requirements are analyzed and documented in terms of a use case model.

The use case model is described in terms of a glossary of terms and a use case model survey description may be prepared. The resulting use case model captures a representation of user requirements. It provides an initial document against which the project scope is determined and a project case is presented if necessary.

The case studies that we present in subsequent chapters include a discussion of the method in which user requirements were collected for the specific case study and have a shallow discussion of a project scope and proposal. However, our main focus is on the process for delivering the modeling artifacts and the deliverables. Consequently the main deliverable of this phase, which will be carried through the subsequent phase, is the use case model.

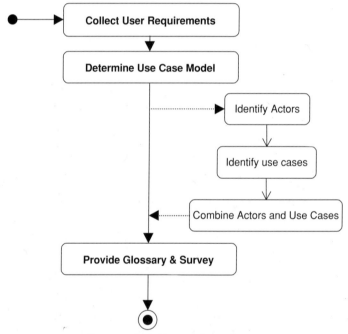

Pattern 2-1. Inception phase

Pattern 2-1 shows the process of achieving the modeling deliverables of this phase. It excludes the activities related to project scope and scope proposal for the reasons mentioned earlier. Determining the use case model follows the following pattern:

Determine user requirements → Identify actors → Identify use cases → Draw the use case model in UML → Prepare a glossary of terms and a survey description of the use case model.

The pattern excludes activities that could also be conducted to reach a project proposal to simplify the presentation. These include steps that validate the resulting use case model with the user before moving to the elaboration phase. We present these for completeness:

——— Not included in Case Studies ———
→ Scope project by interviewing users again → Finalize version 1 of the use case model → Determine project case → Make a project proposal.

3.1 DETERMINING USER REQUIREMENTS

For systems with real users, user requirements may be collected by interviewing users directly, by e-mail, or by any other mechanism.

Objective is to produce a description in user languages that focuses on what the system does and what services need to be automated.

The following are sample questions that could be posed to determine requirements.

- What would the system do? The answer to this question would result in a project description.

- Who would use the system and in what capacity? The answer to the question would determine the different roles of users of the systems.

- What would the users in their different capacities want to get from the system?

In general, questions need to determine general functionality of the system – users and uses of the system, including possible interactions with other existing systems.

Additional nonfunctional requirements may also be collected at this stage, especially those that are critical for proper functioning of the system, such as response time of certain activities.

This activity concludes with a description that states the main objective for developing the system and that captures functions that the system needs to deliver to users and for connectivity to other existing systems. The description could be as simple as the one presented in Figure 2-4, depending on the system to be developed and the thoroughness needed to describe the core functionality of the system.

A software for a wedding agency provides a gift reservation facility for couples who would like to have a wedding list, and a gift purchase facility for people who would like to send gifts. The software keeps information on couples and their corresponding wedding lists. Users can access the system to create or update, cancel, or view their own wedding list, or to buy certain items from a specific wedding list. Users can also get help on how to use the system without the trouble of contacting employees at the wedding agency. Employees at the agency will administrate the system operations. Employees can delete, update, or add items to inventory. Any complaints or suggestions that the client may have could be sent to the agency and stored in a complaint database. To ensure secure access to the system, couples and employees have personal logins and passwords.

Figure 2-4. **Example of user requirements**

3.2 DETERMINING USE CASE MODEL

Determination of the use case model passes through several steps. First, the actors that capture users of the system are identified; next, the use cases that capture uses of the system are determined; then the two are combined into a single use case model.

> **Objective is to produce a use case model that forms the spec-
> ification requirement model of the target software.**

A grammatically based approach is followed to reach the actors, uses, and the formal model systematically.

Identifying Actors

The grammatical approach resolves that all names in user requirements stand for potential actors. This makes it possible to identify all these actors by selecting all the names. The next step would be to filter out eligible actors from the collection of all potential actors that have been determined.

Although the first step is straightforward and automatic, the filtering step carries a factor of subjectivity. The following are guidelines that direct the user in carrying out this process. Out of all potential actors, get rid of the corresponding names that

- do not stand for roles of users. Examples of such names are those that describe attributes or functions of the system. For example, in the description of Figure 2-4, the names wedding list, list and gift do not stand for users of the system so these could be excluded. Also, the name password describes an attribute so it is deleted.

- repetitively describe the same role; in this case, the most descriptive name is kept. For example, in Figure 2-4, people and client stand for the same role, so only one of them is kept.

- are ambiguous. For example, in Figure 2-4, the names system, software, and gift reservation facility may all be deleted because these stand for the system that is still under analysis.

In addition, an analyst may introduce actors that model users of the system and that have not been introduced in user requirements. For instance, an actor called *Database* that holds all information on gift reservations so far may be worth introducing.

This activity concludes with a collection of actors.

Identifying Use Cases

Use cases are determined based on the actors reached in the previous step. All verbs that are associated with actors that have been reached are potential use cases.

After a collection of use cases is determined for each actor, the collection of use cases is revisited according to the following guidelines:

- Only verb phrases that describe uses of the system are kept; others are deleted.

- Repetitive verb phrases or those that describe similar uses are deleted; the most appropriate verb phrase is kept.

- Ambiguous and redundant verb phrases are also deleted. For example, in Figure 2-4, the verb uses in the verb phrase *How to use the system* could be deleted since determining use cases is the process in which all of these uses are found.

- If no appropriate verb phrases were found, then new descriptions of behavior of actors may be introduced from which use cases could be determined in a similar manner.

- For actors that stand for boundary systems, use cases that describe interactions with the system are identified in the same manner.

This activity concludes with a collection of use cases for each actor, which was determined in the previous activity.

Draw First Version of the Use Case Model in UML Notation

Actors and use cases are collected and organized into a use case model. This activity is straightforward but concludes with a diagrammatic representation of user requirements that captures the core functionality of the system.

3.3 GIVING A GLOSSARY

A glossary attempts to define the meaning of each actor. The glossary focuses on roles of using the system and takes into consideration the system context. For instance, the name client could have different meanings in different system contexts. The most appropriate definition needs to be stated.

> **Objective is to produce a description for each actor that defines the meaning of the actor in the context of the target system.**

Providing a glossary has the following advantages:

- A glossary provides a common vocabulary between developers and real users. It is the nonformal description of the specification model captured by the use case model.

- A glossary provides new content that could lead to additional use cases and potential actors which were not introduced in the description of user requirements but are relevant to the software domain.

This phase could be concluded with a validation activity during which the user is consulted. The objective is to verify that the initial use case model and glossary do capture the target software system. Performing this activity at this stage is worthwhile because it permits detection of invalid uses or users early in the development cycle and carries over any modifications that may be found to be essential.

> **This phase concludes with a use case model and a glossary**

4. ELABORATION

The **elaboration** phase consists of mostly analysis with initial design. During this phase four key activities are performed in the following order:

1. *Requirements Analysis:* based on one or more refined versions of the initial use case model. The final version gives a semiformal model of the system.

2. *Domain Analysis:* an initial object design model is derived. The derivation of the object model is considered to be an analysis activity but sets the stage for design in the construction phase.

3. *Subsystems Analysis:* an initial division of the software in terms of subsystems. The derivation of the system model in terms of subsystems is also considered to be a step toward commencing design activity.

4. *Traceability:* This step concludes the phase with a detailed use case analysis that determines traces among deliverables of the three activities. This activity is a preamble for deriving the final use case model. The word final in this context means the produced models would be carried through to the next phase.

The deliverables of this phase are summarized in Figure 2-5.

4.1 REQUIREMENTS ANALYSIS

This activity is a refinement of the use case model reached in the inception phase. During this activity the use case model may be refined at least once to produce a preliminary final use case model that contains interfaces, extends relations, and generalization relations. Activity diagrams that model instantiation of use cases are also produced.

> **Objective is to produce a semiformal specification model expressed in terms of a use case model that captures services and functionality of the system.**

Elaboration	Deliverables
Requirements Analysis	Primary Scenarios Activity Diagrams Use Case Model Version 2 Secondary Scenarios Use Case Model Version 3
Domain Analysis	Object Model
Subsystem Analysis	Subsystem Model
Traceability	Trace Model

Figure 2-5. **Deliverables of the elaboration phase**

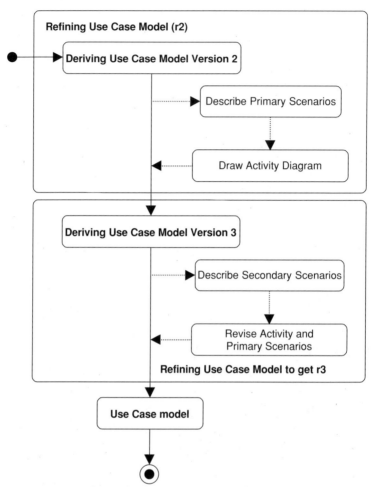

Pattern 2-2. Requirement analysis

Pattern 2-2 shows a detailed pattern activity diagram for the process of performing requirements analysis. The case studies of this book instantiate Pattern 2-3, which is a simplified version of Pattern 2-2. The key difference is that Pattern 2-2 allows for revising and refining use case models with the introduction of each new analysis detail, permitting capture of all details immediately in the use case model. Pattern 2-3 is suitable for simple cases. It allows performance of the key steps to produce deliverables necessary to reach a use case model. Note that the final version of the use case model that starts the construction phase is determined at the beginning of that phase.

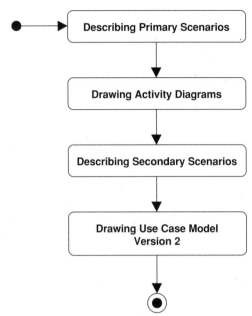

***Pattern 2-3.* Requirements analysis (simplified version)**

Determining Primary Scenarios

A primary scenario gives a detailed description of a use case. A description consists of how a use case starts, what an actor could achieve from the system, how it ends, and a pre- and postcondition.

A precondition defines the condition that needs to be satisfied for the activity described in the body of the use case to be performed. The body consists of a sequence of actions that could be performed by an actor of the system. The actions may be listed sequentially or with conditionals that need to be satisfied for the actions to be done. Repetitive actions may be included in a while loop. Figure 2-6 shows a generic layout of a use case description.

Name of primary scenario
Precondition
    Body:
        Sequence of activities that make the scenarios *including*
        Conditions with branches or repetition
Postcondition

***Figure 2-6.* Format for describing scenarios**

Determining Secondary Scenarios

Secondary scenarios express exceptions to the normal sequence of events determined by primary scenarios. These typically focus on behaviors related to nonfunctional requirements and are expressed after the postconditions.

Determining Activity Diagrams

This step results in producing activity diagrams for the use cases in the resulting use case model. An activity diagram consists of an initial state and a final state and a sequence of intermediate states that may include branching and looping.

To determine activity diagrams:

- For each primary scenario and each step in this scenario, consider the most descriptive verb phrases. Each of these verb phrases corresponds to an intermediate state.

- Join the states following the same order of description in the scenarios.

- Model loops in one state with an arrow from the state to itself and general repetitions with backward arrows.

- Model conditionals with branching arrows to one or more states.

- Determine the initial state and model the initial state using a black rounded ball.

- Determine all the final states. Each terminating state is a final state. Model final states with the bull's-eye notation.

Use Case Model

Pattern 2-2 shows a detailed analysis in which two intermediate refinements of the use case model are reached that result in the second and third versions of the use case model obtained from the requirements analysis phase.

The second version of the use case model (version r2) is obtained from the activity diagrams that are derived from the primary scenarios.

When the activity diagrams are reached, join each activity diagram to the actor to which the corresponding use case was associated. The resulting diagrammatic model will be the second refined version of the use case model.

Refining the Use Case Model

The second refinement results in the third version (r3) of the use case model:

- First, secondary scenarios are introduced.

- Next, primary scenarios are revised to account for secondary scenarios. In addition, the primary scenarios are studied and refined so that the commonalities are expressed as independent use cases and the scenarios are related, if applicable, by extends and generalization relationships. The finalized primary scenarios are refined to include possible alternative paths or nonfunctional requirements.

- The activity diagrams produced earlier may be revisited now to be updated according to modifications made to primary scenarios.

- The third version of the use case model is obtained from version 2 and in relation to the relationship derived earlier. The model is drawn in UML.

Adding Interfaces

An interface may be added between each actor and use case. Actors may use the same interface to access the same use case(s); alternatively, a single interface can connect an actor to several use cases. An interface needs to be added between use cases and passive actors, such as other external systems.

Interfaces are added to the final use case model. To determine the position of interfaces versus use cases, use the following:

- For every use case relation determine the input needed for the use case to follow and complete the activities at least in the primary scenarios.

- If the same input is needed for several activities then introduce one interface notation at the entry point to the activities.

- Describing inputs for each use case helps to determine the most appropriate position for the activity diagrams.

This subphase concludes with the second version of the use case model.

4.2 DOMAIN ANALYSIS

This phase is the first phase in the design activity. The main deliverable of this phase is the object model, which consists of class programming abstractions related by associations. Also, attributes and methods may be specified inside classes at this stage.

Objective is to produce an object model that gives an initial design of the target system.

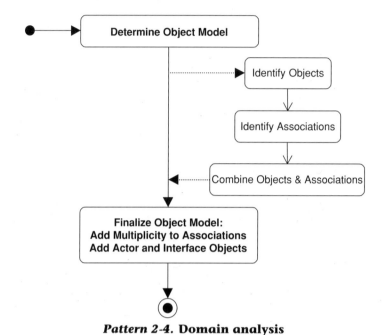

Pattern 2-4. Domain analysis

Pattern 2-4 shows the main steps in analyzing the software domain to reach the initial object model: first objects are determined, then associations, then the model is drafted from the resulting objects and associations. Finally multiplicity, attributes, and initial methods may be added to conclude with an initial object model.

We distinguish among three kinds of objects: first, boundary objects that capture the behavior of actors; second, interface objects that capture interfaces between actors and use cases; and third, business or domain objects that capture the functionality of the system. Boundary and interface objects could be derived from the use case model directly. In fact, one programming abstraction could be added to model each of these objects after the initial model is derived.

Determining the Objects

To determine domain objects we use the following steps, which are adapted to the bridge process from the OMT methodology.

The objects may be derived from user requirements, the glossary, or the survey description, which, as mentioned earlier, are expected to closely correspond to one another. Objects in the initial object model correspond to a subset of the names in the survey description or user requirements. To determine all the objects use the following steps:

- Select all the names.

- Eliminate names that are attribute-like. For example, password is more like an attribute than an object.

- Eliminate duplicate names or different names that appear but have the same meaning, keeping only one. For example, if the names customer, client, and user appear in the same context then it is enough to keep one to indicate potential clients or users of the system

- Eliminate ambiguous names. For example, software system could be eliminated because the whole model refers to the system.

- Eliminate names that are close to implementation. For example, a name like *access language* that refers to the programming language could be deleted at this stage.

- Add names that would represent useful objects.

- The remaining names correspond to object names. Some of these objects would correspond to actors; the remaining would be initial business objects.

- Add interface objects.

Determining Associations

The associations among objects correspond to a subset of the verbs in the survey description of the use case model or user requirements. To determine the associations, use the following:

- Select all the verb phrases in the user requirement.

- Eliminate from the selected verb phrases all verb phrases that relate objects that have been previously excluded when determining the objects.

- The remaining verb phrases fall into several categories: associations, generalizations, or consist relations. Any verb phrase that describes containment corresponds to an aggregation, an is-a verb describes generalizations, and the remaining are associations.

- Examine each of the remaining relationships to determine multiplicity on both ends of the relation.

Determining Attributes

Some of the attributes could be derived from names that were eliminated when determining the objects. Usually the attributes added at this stage are related to the core function of the objects, such as name and password. The types of the attributes need to be general and avoid commitment to implementation detail. An appropriate approach would be to confine the types to general class names or standard types. Also, using container classes with generic types for capturing containers such as lists, arrays, or tables would be appropriate.

Drawing the Object Model

Combine the resulting objects, associations, and attributes to reach the object model. Use UML notation to draw the resulting model.

This section concludes with the initial object model.

4.3 SUBSYSTEM ANALYSIS

Objective is to identify the components of the target system and their communication.

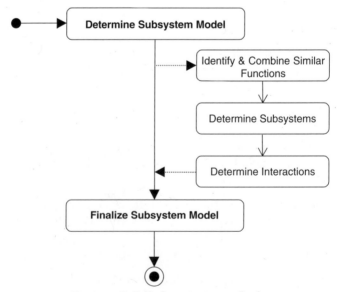

Pattern 2-5. Subsystem analysis

This activity results in identifying the main subsystems and interfaces among these subsystems. The resulting model is the first version of what is commonly referred to in the literature as the architecture. We call it the subsystem model to distinguish it from the architectural model of the UML process.

To determine the subsystem model we go through the following steps (see Pattern 2-5).

- Identify the main functions of the system as captured in user requirements. Group objects with similar functionality together. These will probably provide the main subsystems.

- Interactions among the subsystems can be determined from the activity diagrams, as follows:
  - For each transition of an activity diagram identify the client object that owns the source state. Then map the client object to the corresponding subsystem.
  - Similarly, for each transition determine the target object that owns the target state of a transition. Then map the target object to the corresponding subsystem.
  - The transition between the source and target state captures an interaction between the subsystems of the target and source objects. If the source and target states belong to the same subsystem then the interaction is internal to the subsystem. Alternatively it is an external communication between the subsystems.

- Draw the resulting subsystems and direction of interactions.

- Document your architecture by describing the functions of the subsystem and how they interact.

This section concludes the initial subsystem model.

4.4 TRACEABILITY

Objective: This activity establishes traces among the deliverables of activities of the elaboration phase and validates these deliverables against user requirements.

A *trace* is a relation between two artifacts that determines how one deliverable can be derived from another. Based on the resulting traces the object and subsystem models may be modified to add new objects, associations, and interactions.

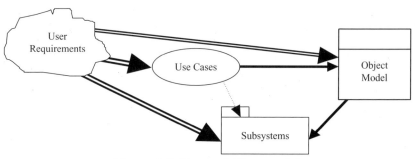

***Figure 2-7.* Traceability model**

In this activity two kinds of traces are determined:

- Use case model to the object model through a detailed use case analysis.
- Object model to the model.

Three tables are generated that summarize the results of these activities.

Figure 2-7 shows the relationship between the two trace activities. The double arrow means derives; the single arrows model traceability between use case and object models and between object model and model, respectively. The dashed arrow models the transitivity relation of traceability from user requirements, as well as from the use case model, to the architecture model.

Note the double arrows. The double arrow from User Requirements to Object Model indicates that the object model is derived directly from the requirements, as introduced in the elaboration phase. Similarly the double arrow from User Requirements to the Use Case model indicates that the use case model is derived directly from user requirements. A third double arrow between User Requirements and Subsystems also indicates that the latter was derived directly from user requirements.

The bridge process bridges the gap between the analysis model captured by the use case model and the object model by one of the trace activities. The other trace activity captures a similar gap between the object model and the model. Once the two traces are established, the third discrepancy between the use case model and the model follows by a transitivity relation.

Use Cases to Objects: Detailed Use Case Analysis

In this activity a detailed use case analysis is performed. This is achieved by tracing use cases through objects in the object model obtained in the domain analysis activity. As a consequence new associations that establish this trace are added to the object model.

The trace is determined by reliance on the activity diagrams. Each of these diagrams is an instantiation of a use case. Tracing these diagrams through the object model and determining the objects traced would verify that a use case model could be implemented in the object model.

The trace is determined as follows for each diagram:

- Map each state in the activity diagram to an object in the object model.

- Map each following transition to an association in the object model. Two possibilities arise.

    First, the transition may turn to model a behavior internal to the object to which the state was mapped then add an incoming association to the object.

    Second, the transition may model an outgoing behavior then add an outgoing association to the object model. This may result in a large number of associations added to the object model. In this case it might be more appropriate to keep the resulting associations in a table so that they would be considered in the subsequent phases.

Results of traceability activities may be summarized for clarity and later implementation purposes (see Tables 2-1 and 2-2).

use case	step of use case	client object	supplier object

Table 2-1. **A summary of all objects traversed by a single use case**

Use Case Name	Objects crossed by use case in order of traversal

Table 2-2. **A summary of all objects traversed by a single use case**

It might be worth warning the reader that the described trace activity could be tiring. However, it has the advantage of verifying correctness between preliminary versions of the design and user requirements that have been captured in the use case model.

Objects to Architecture

This activity establishes a relationship between the object model and the derived subsystem architecture. This is done by assigning each object in the object model to one of the subsystems. The assignment may be established systematically by looking for the object names in the subsystem descriptions. Objects whose names appear in more than one system's description are considered to be interface objects. A table with headings similar to the one in Table 2-3 could be used to summarize results of this trace activity for use in subsequent examples.

Object name	Subsystem name

Table 2-3. **A summary of all objects traversed by a single use case**

5. CONSTRUCTION SUBPHASE 1

Subphase 1 of construction finalizes the requirements model and focuses mostly on design and initiates implementation. The requirements model is finalized by revisiting the final use case model and modifying it in lieu of the trace established in the last activity of the elaboration phase. Typically the modifications of the requirements model are minimal. However, asserting it as a final model gives an assuring background for the remaining design and implementation activities. The addition of interfaces also could be done at this stage.

The object model is refined so that design classes such as container classes, proxies, and interface classes are determined. The detailed design is supposed to be obtained iteratively from the first version of the object model by adding design classes and integrating the associations into the object model. In addition, the interfaces of classes are detailed and described in terms of attributes, functions, and interface links. Also, the described subsystem model is detailed into a physical architecture. This subphase concludes with a traceability section that maps the last version of the deliverables (use case and object design) to one another and to user requirements.

5.1 USE CASES REVISITED

The use case model is reviewed. The revisions and consequent modifications need to be guided by the traces determined in the elaboration phase; new association may be added to states among use case models with extra possibilities. In addition, the interfaces that were identified in version 3 of the model are prototyped and an initial version is produced. The use case model is by and large finalized at this stage and determines the project scope including interactions with other existing systems.

5.2 DYNAMIC MODELING

This activity captures the dynamic behavior of objects in terms of sequence and collaboration diagrams.

Sequence diagrams capture dynamic behavior of objects in terms of lifelines and messages and these could be derived from primary scenarios.

For each primary scenario:

– Select objects that are involved in performing the scenario.

– For each such object, introduce a class abstraction and corresponding lifeline

– For each step in the primary scenario select the two objects that are involved in performing this step. Next draw a message (represented with an arrow) from the lifeline of the client object to the lifeline of the supplier object. If the client and supplier object are the same represent the message with a loop. Position the messages on the lifelines in the order in which they correspond to steps in the scenario.

Collaboration diagrams are similar to state activity diagrams. A diagram consists of classes and transitions between classes. Collaboration diagrams could be derived directly using UML from sequence diagrams.

5.3 DETAILED OBJECT DESIGN

Objective: The deliverable of this activity is a detailed object design diagram.

This activity refines the object model obtained in the elaboration phase. The refinement is done to include inheritance relations and then introduce design attributes, design classes, and methods.

This activity is considered to be the beginning of some implementation decisions related to the type of the attributes, performance, and other decisions.

Noting that a substantial aspect of the design can be guided by the associations relating objects in the object model, the following are guidelines for reaching design versions of the object model.

Design of Inheritance Relations

We study the object model to abstract common generalization classes and express these using inheritance relation.

Design of One-to-One Associations

Each one to-one association results in introducing an attribute definition in the client class and a method in the target supplier class of the association. The type of the added attribute is the supplier class.

For example, in Figure 2-8, the one-to-one association between class *Employee* and class *Company* is implemented as an attribute C, whose type is *Company*, and a function *works-for* in class *Company*.

Design of One-to-Many Associations

By one-to-many associations, we mean associations that express a one-to-many relationship between a client and supplier. For example, relations such as the following are appropriately captured by a one-to-many association: A person has accounts at several banks; a student has memberships at several fitness clubs.

One-to-many associations could contribute to the design as follows. Introduce a Container (could be a data structure) class with a generic parameter. Add one entity in the client class with data type the container class instantiated with the supplier class. Introduce an entity or a method to the supplier

(a) 1-1 association from the analysis model

Employee	works for	Company

(b) The corresponding design model

Employee		Company
Company C		
		works-for()

Figure 2-8. **An example of a design of a one-to-one association**

(a) 1-many association from the analysis model

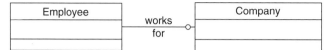

Figure 2-9. A one-to-many association

(b) The Corresponding design model

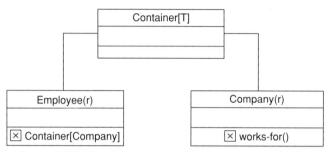

Figure 2-10. Design of a one-to-many association

class to implement the association. The choice of the kind of the container at this stage may be left open because finalizing such a decision could be postponed to the implementation. Figure 2-9 shows one example of a one-to-many association, and Figure 2-10 shows one possible design.

Note that the container class may be replaced by a database that contains data on the company class.

Many-to-Many Associations

Many-to-many associations express many-to-many relations. These are described with multiplicity notation on both sides of the association. Design-wise, two approaches could be followed:

- The association is implemented as an independent container generic class of two parameters. A table data structure would be appropriate. One of the generic parameters would be instantiated with the client, the other with the supplier.

An attribute is added to each of the client and supplier classes such that the type of each attribute is the container class instantiated with the client and

(a) Many-to-many association from the analysis model

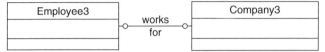

Figure 2-11. A many-to-many association

(b) The corresponding design model

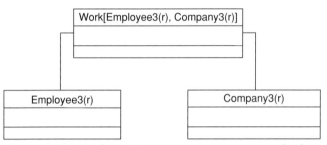

Figure 2-12. Design of a many-to-many association

supplier classes. See the example in Figures 2-11 and 2-12. Figures 2-11 and 2-12 show a many-to-many association and one possible design.

An alternative design may treat the association in Figure 2-11 as if it were two independent one-to-many associations resulting in two instantiated container classes whose actual parameters are the client and the supplier classes. The association would be added as a method to the supplier. Also, two attributes whose types are the newly introduced classes are added, one to the client, the other to the supplier class. The first solution typically results in more modular implementations because any changes would affect the implementation class.

Aggregations

Aggregations model the "consist" relation. Consequently, the aggregation design results in introduction of one attribute for each aggregate class. Then each of the involved relations is designed in the same way as normal associations.

Figure 2-13 shows an aggregation relation, and Figure 2-14 shows a corresponding design model. Note that the design added three attributes *l*, *t*, and *c* of types *ChoiceList*, *TextArea*, and *Button*, which correspond to the constituent classes. A container class and corresponding attribute was also added between classes *Panel* and *Button* as a result of the multiplicity of the association relating these classes.

(a) An aggregation from the analysis model

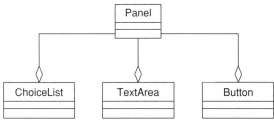

Figure 2-13. An aggregation

(b) The corresponding design model

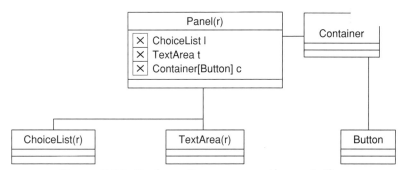

Figure 2-14. Design of an aggregation relation

Design from Nonfunctional Requirements

Some nonfunctional requirements may require introducing attributes or classes. For example, derived attributes and corresponding classes may be introduced as data repositories for speed purposes. A class may be introduced to record the results of time-consuming operations that do not change frequently. Data can then be browsed repeatedly without the need to repeat the calculations.

Figures 2-15 and 2-16 illustrate this concept. Assume that the university is interested in frequently referring to data on students on probation. These data are computed once at the beginning of a semester and are kept or accessed directly through class probation throughout the semester. Consequently a designer would introduce one *Container* class to keep these data, as shown in Figure 2-16.

(a) An association from the analysis model

Figure 2-15. University student association

(b) The corresponding design classes

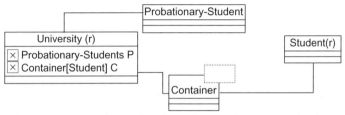

Figure 2-16. Design of university student association

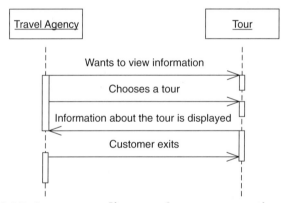

Figure 2-17. A sequence diagram from a reservation system

Design from Sequence or Collaboration Diagrams

Sequence diagrams provide an interesting source of operation and method design. This activity may be performed for objects with complicated behavior. Consider the lifeline that corresponds to an object in a sequence diagram.

Each outgoing arrow could be designed in terms of an attribute in the client and a method in the supplier such that the attribute has the the supplier as a type.

Consider the state diagram in Figure 2-17. It has two classes, *TravelAgency* and *Tour*. The message passing among objects indicates that there needs to be a means for communication between objects of the two classes. This could be accounted for by having an attribute of type *Tour* in class *TravelAgency* and another whose type is *TravelAgency* in class *Tour*. A message such as *Wants to view information* could be designed as an operation *ViewInformation* in class *Tour*. Similarly, the message *Chooses a tour* could be designed as an operation *ChooseATour* in class *Tour*.

5.4 TRACEABILITY

This activity is similar to the traceability activity of the elaboration phase. In this phase we again establish traces between objects in the detailed object model and use cases. Traces are also established between objects and the subsystem model.

Use Cases to Objects

Recall the modified scenarios and activity diagrams (in case of any modification) or the original ones described for the use cases. For each step of each scenario of a use case, map the use case to an association in the detailed object model. If no such association is present, add the association. Give a table that summarizes this mapping, as shown in Table 2-4.

Use case name	Step in the use case	Client object	Supplier object

Table 2-4. **A summary of all objects traversed by a single use case**

For each use case identify the sequence of objects in the new object model (version 2) that the use case would cross. The activity diagrams should guide you in this. Summarize the results in a table, as shown in Table 2-5.

Use Case name	Objects crossed by the use case in order of traversal

Table 2-5. **A summary of all objects traversed by a single use case**

Objects to Architecture

Consider the object model obtained in Section 3.3. Assign each object to one of the subsystems in the architecture of Section 2. Give a table that summarizes this assignment, as shown in Table 2-6.

Object Name	Subsystem Name

Table 2-6. **A summary of all objects traversed by a single use case**

The trace activity from state activity diagrams to objects introduces new associations. Consequently, it helps to identify additional attributes and methods. Also, the trace activity from objects to subsystems introduces new interactions among objects in the same and in distinct subsystems.

6. CONSTRUCTION SUBPHASE 2

The second subphase of construction, by and large, finalizes the design and proceeds toward implementation. In lieu of our focus stated earlier and our introduction to focus on the first three subphases, we briefly summarize key steps of this phase without detail.

In this subphase, state diagrams are produced and classes are implemented as a consequence. This phase may include a description of programming language, an environment of one possible implementation.

Implementation design, including implementing operations, has been identified. The object implementation design process could precede implementation. In addition, the design activity could extend to designing an algorithm of the identified operations.

Object Implementation

Object implementation may be guided by state diagrams as follows.

Give state diagrams for sequence diagrams as well as objects for which the implementation of the objects' behavior is not straightforward because of the active behavior of the object.

For each state diagram in Section 4.1, give code that implements the state diagram.

Algorithm Design

Choose algorithms for the methods that have been identified. These algorithms should be chosen to be simple, flexible (i.e., easy to change), and efficient. If any of these criteria conflict with each other then choose the ones that are consistent with priorities set for the project. For example, if one priority is reusable code, then choose simple and flexible algorithms even if they are not efficient.

7. CONCLUSION

This chapter introduced the bridge process. It described how it would be possible to design a software system rigorously and systematically starting from user requirements.

Part II

Developed Case Studies

This part introduces two case studies taken from two different problem domains. The first case study has an internet-based architecture and is an interesting model to apply to applications that deal with reservations; the second deals with web development. This application has a network-based architecture and could also be used as a model to develop similar applications. The bridge process is applied in detail including details of traceability. Both could be viewed as tutorials on applying the bridge process and could be used as such to guide the reader in solving the exercises at the end of the chapters in Part III.

Chapter 3

Reservations Online: Case Study 1

Work on this case study was motivated by an antici-
pated need of travel agencies to improve their sales by
making their products, namely, tours, directly accessible
to their client base. Although this application focuses on
travel agencies, it could be viewed as one instantiation
of a general application framework that handles reser-
vations in general, such as hotel and car reservations.

1. INCEPTION

1.1 USER REQUIREMENTS

User requirements are a summary of information that is collected by customers asking travel agencies about tours that the travel agencies offer. From
that information we deduced the user requirements, shown in Description
3-1.

Constraints

For simplicity, we made two assumptions. The first one is that the customer
can only reserve a single tour. Consequently, he is assigned a login ID and a
password. The second assumption is that the customer can optionally reserve
as many trips as he wants in his tour reservation. For example, suppose that

A software for a travel agency provides reservation facilities for the people who
wish to travel on tours by accessing a built-in network at the agency bureau.
The application software keeps information on tours. Users can access the
system to make a reservation on a tour and to view information about the tours
available without having to go through the trouble of asking the employees at
the agency. The third option is to cancel a reservation that he/she made.

Any complaints or suggestions that the client may have could be sent by
e-mail to the agency or stored in a complaint database. Finally, the employees
of the corresponding agency could use the application to administrate the
system's operations. Employees could add, delete, and update the information
on the customers and the tours. For security purposes, the employee should
be provided a login ID and password by the manager to be able to access the
database of the travel agency.

Description 3-1. Tours Online user requirements

the travel agency company provides a tour to Athens. Then the customer
who chooses this tour can optionally choose one or more trips related to the
Athens tour such as a trip to the temples or a tour to Olympus.

1.2 USE CASE MODEL (VERSION 1)

Actors

For determining actors we will consider all the names in Description 3-1 then
eliminate those names that do not stand for roles of users of the system. The
elimination would also include names that describe the same role. Names
that describe roles of users most adequately are kept as shown in Table 3-1.

Travel agency
Software
People
Built in network
Agency
Application software
Client
Customer
Tour
Employee
Manager

Table 3-1. List of names in user requirements

Table 3-1 shows all the names from the user requirements that could possibly identify actors. All names in this table are eliminated except for two names that we identify as actors of the system for the following reasons: We selected the word employee due to the meaning that it represents. With this word, we have represented the travel agency and all its employees including the manager. So employee was chosen to be the first user of the system. The words software and application software are just descriptive words and, as a result, they were not considered actors or users of the system. The second actor was identified to be the client or the customer. Both words correspond to the same behavior; we chose customer because it is more descriptive. The word tour describes the purpose of this software, that is, to be able to reserve a tour, so it is not considered an actor. Finally, the word agency was excluded because it is a repetition of travel agency. The behavior of both is captured in the employee actor.

Determining Use Cases

To obtain use cases, we consider the verb phrases in the user requirements (Description 3-1) that are associated with selected actors. Table 3-2 gives a summary of all verb phrases. Only those associated with actors are kept.

~~Provides reservation~~	~~wish~~	~~keeps information~~
~~can access~~	make a reservation	view information
Cancel a reservation	could be sent	~~stored~~
Administrate	~~add~~	~~delete~~
~~Update access~~		

Table 3-2. **List of verbs in the user requirements**

The verbs that are not crossed out in Table 3-2 are sufficient to model uses of the system as follows.

Employee uses the software to "add, delete, and update the information concerning the customers and the tours." **Customer** uses the system to "reserve one tour," to "view information about the tours available . . . ," and to "cancel any of the reservation done by the customer." Moreover, it includes "any complaints or suggestions that the client may have to be sent through the mail to the agency or stored in its database."

As a result, we have decided on five use cases, which are **Reserving, Canceling, Viewing Information, Complaining** (by sending an e-mail), and **Administrate. Reserving, Viewing Information**, and **Canceling and Complaining** are for customer actors. The other actor, **Employee**, will use

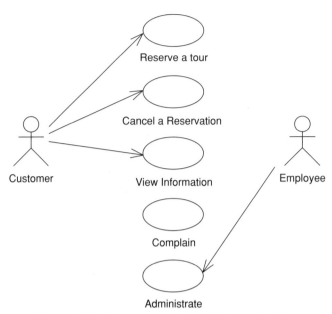

Reserve a tour

Cancel a Reservation

Customer   **View Information**   Employee

Complain

Administrate

***Figure 3-1.* Use case model of Tours Online**

the system through the **Administrate** option. This word summarizes the three actions of the employee, that is, adding, deleting, and updating information.

Figure 3-1 shows an initial use case model composed of the obtained actors and cases.

Employee and Customer are the only actors: Employee captures the behavior of all possible users of the system including the agency manager. Customer captures behavior of all possible clients. This model captures a view of the required system and generates functionality that will be supported.

Glossary

Customer: represents the client of the travel agency who will use the system to reserve a tour, view information about the tours available, or cancel any of the reservation he/she has already made. Finally, customers could file their complaints or suggestions to the agency by e-mail.

Employee: represents the staff of the travel agency who will have the ability to add, delete, and update any information concerning the customers and the tours.

***Description 3-2.* Tours Online glossary of actors**

Output of this phase is the preliminary use case model (Figure 3-1) and the glossary (Description 3-2).

2. ELABORATION

2.1 REQUIREMENTS ANALYSIS

In this phase, the intial use case model captured in Figure 3-1 is developed through a somewhat detailed analysis of use cases. The analysis is captured using activity diagrams.

2.1.1 Primary Scenarios

This section describes one primary scenario for each use case in the use case model. Determining the primary scenario is based on the conception of how the system may behave coupled with input from the analysts with regard to a real user. Each scenario clarifies and details one use case. Consequently, scenarios are part of the user requirements. In addition, we find it appropriate to introduce a scenario that begins to capture the startup activity of the system by reading the specific functionality. The administrate use case was very comprehensive of all activities of employee. For simplicity, we chose to give a scenario for one instance of this activity.

1. NAME: STARTING. (*ACTIVITY DIAGRAM 3-1*)

Precondition: Customer started the application.
The customer selects one of the available choices:
a) View information.
b) Reserve in a tour.
c) Cancel a reservation.
d) Administrate.
e) Complain.
f) Exit.
Postcondition: A choice is made.

Scenario 3-1

2. NAME: RESERVING. (*ACTIVITY DIAGRAM 3-2*)

Precondition: The customer chose "Reserve" a tour.
1. The system displays information on tours.
2. The customer enters a login ID.
3. The customer chooses a tour.
4. The customer selects a hotel.
5. If the customer selects "trips" then
    a) A list of trips available for the chosen tour is displayed.
    b) Customer chooses as many trips as he wants.
    End
6. The customer fills out a form with the following data: customer's name, age, sex, address, occupation, phone number, and e-mail if available.
7. The system provides the customer with the cost of the tour and the whole preview.
8. The customer selects Submit.
9. Reservation is marked confirmed and a customer login ID is returned to the customer for confirmation.
Postcondition: The user has reserved a place on a tour.

Scenario 3-2

3. NAME: VIEWING INFORMATION. (*ACTIVITY DIAGRAM 3-3*)

Precondition: The customer chose "view information."
1. The customer chooses the tour he/she wants to know about.
2. The information is displayed from the database.
3. The customer exits from the system.
Postcondition: The customer has obtained information.

Scenario 3-3

4. NAME: CANCELING A RESERVATION. (*ACTIVITY DIAGRAM 3-4*)

Precondition: The customer chose the "Cancel" option from the menu.
1. The customer enters his/her login ID.
2. The customer selects the Cancel button.
3. The customer submits the form.
4. The customer exits the system.
Postcondition: The reservation is cancelled.

Scenario 3-4

5. NAME: EMPLOYEES' INTERACTION: RETRIEVE INFORMATION AS ONE INSTANCE OF ADMINISTRATE. *(ACTIVITY DIAGRAM 3-5)*

Precondition: The employee of the travel agency chose "Administrate" to retrieve information about the customers
1. The employee enters his/her employee login with his/her password.
2. The employee presses Submit.
3. A list of currently available tours is displayed.
4. The employee selects the tour he/she wants.
5. The system will display the information about all the customers in this tour.
6. The employee logs out.

Postcondition: The employee has data on the customers.

Scenario 3-5

6. NAME: REGISTERING A COMPLAINT. *(ACTIVITY DIAGRAM 3-6)*

Precondition: The customer chose "Complain."
1. A description form is displayed.
2. The customer writes the complaint.
3. The customer previews the complaint.
4. The customer submits the form.
5. The telephone numbers of the tour company are displayed for advanced information.

Postcondition: The complaint is stored in the database.

Scenario 3-6

2.1.2 Secondary Scenarios

We present possible secondary scenarios in this section. Each scenario is associated with one of the previously described primary scenarios. Other secondary scenarios may be added that may vary with security, robustness, and other nonfunctional requirements of the system.

Name: Running Problems.
Primary Scenario: Starting.
The customer was not able to run the application (either due to an error in the application itself or because of some networking problem).

Name: Incomplete Reservation.
Primary Scenario: Reserving.

The customer tries to submit an incomplete reservation form, such as one missing the tour name, hotel name, login, or ID form. For each incomplete part of the reservation form an error message box will appear.

Name: Reservation Got Lost.
Primary Scenario: Reserving.
Due to an error in connections, the information about the reservation is lost.

Name: Invalid Login.
Primary Scenario: Canceling a reservation.
The customer wants to cancel a reservation. The customer enters an incorrect login (different from the one he/she chose). An error message appears prompting the customer to write his/her login correctly or (in case it was forgotten) to go and retrieve the login after entering his/her first name and last name and the tour name.

Name: Invalid Login and Password.
Primary Scenario: Employees interaction.
The employee entered a wrong login or password when wanting to access the administrator page. An error message will appear, asking him/her to correct the error.

Name: E-mail Server Down.
Primary Scenario: Registering a complaint.
The customer tries to send an e-mail complaint but the e-mail server is down.

Name: Optional Reservation.
Primary Scenario: Reserving.
The customer selects one or more additional round trips in the countries.

2.1.3 Activity Diagrams

Figures 3-2 to 3-7 gives the activity diagrams of primary scenarios 3-1 to 3-6 respectively. To draw the activity diagrams, we followed the steps of primary scenarios. For each step we identified the phrase that best describes an activity of the system. Each activity was used to name a state in a corresponding activity diagram. For clarity, primary scenarios are repeated and selected verb phrases and, consequently, anticipated states are in bold and underlined.

1. STARTING ACTIVITY

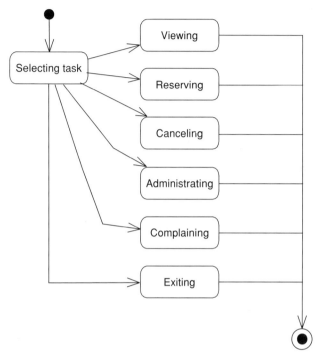

Figure 3-2. **Starting Tours Online**

Precondition: The customer started the application.
The user **selects** one of the available choices:
a) **View** information.
b) **Reserve** in a tour.
c) **Cancel** a reservation.
d) **Administrate**.
e) **Complain**.
f) **Exit**.
Postcondition: A choice is made.

2. RESERVING ACTIVITY

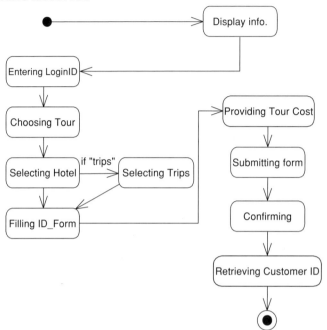

Figure 3-3. Reserving

Precondition: Customer chose "Reserve" a tour.
1. The system **displays information** on tours.
2. The customer **enters a login ID**.
3. The customer **chooses a tour**.
4. The customer **selects a hotel**.
5. If the customer **selects "trips"** then
     a) A list of available trips corresponding to the chosen tour is displayed.
     b) The customer chooses as many trips as he/she wants.
     End
6. The customer **fills out a form** with the following data: customer's name, age, sex, address, occupation, phone number, and e-mail if available.
7. The system **provides** the customer with the **cost of the tour** and the whole preview.
8. The customer selects **Submit**.
9. **Reservation is marked confirmed** and the customer **login ID is returned** to the customer for confirmation.
Postcondition: The user has reserved a place on a tour.

3. VIEWING INFORMATION ACTIVITY

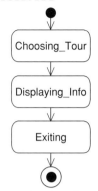

Figure 3-4. Viewing information

Precondition: The customer chose "view information."
1. The customer **chooses the tour** he/she wants to know about.
2. The **information is displayed** from the database.
3. The customer **exits** from the system.
Postcondition: The customer has obtained information.

4. CANCELING ACTIVITY

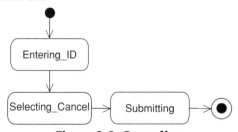

Figure 3-5. Canceling

Precondition: The customer chose the "Cancel" option from the menu.
1. The customer enters his/her **login ID**.
2. The customer **selects the Cancel** button.
3. The customer **submits the form**.
4. The customer **exits** the system.
Postcondition: The reservation is cancelled.

5. ADMINISTRATE ACTIVITY

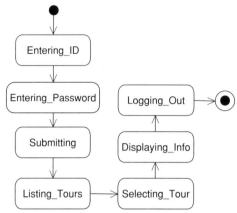

Figure 3-6. **Administrate**

> **Precondition:** The employee of the travel agency chose "Administrate" to retrieve information about the customers.
> 1. The employee **enters his/her login Id with his password.**
> 2. The employee presses **Submit**.
> 3. A list of currently **available tours is displayed**.
> 4. The employee **selects the tour** he/she wants.
> 5. The system will **display the information** about all the customers in this tour.
> 6. The employee **logs out**.
> **Postcondition:** The employee has data on the customers.

6. COMPLAINING ACTIVITY

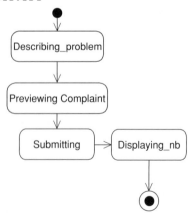

Figure 3-7. **Complaining**

Precondition: The customer chose "Complain."
1. A description form is displayed.
2. The customer **writes the complaint**.
3. The customer **previews the complaint**.
4. The customer **submits** the form.
5. The **telephone numbers** of the tour company **are displayed** for advanced information.

Postcondition: The complaint is stored in the database.

2.2 DOMAIN ANALYSIS: DERIVING THE INITIAL OBJECT MODEL

Figure 3-8 is an object model obtained from the requirements in Description 3-1. Seven objects are identified that correspond to names in the user requirements. The names that are left out are considered to be redundant or too general to be considered at this stage. For example, *software, network, facilities, choices, operation,* and *option* are very general. *People, client,* and *users* all refer to **customer**. *Bureau* refers to travel agency. By comparing Figures 3-1 and 3-8, we note how the customer and actor employees reappear as objects in the object model. Note as well how the use cases are modeled as functions in main object of the application or as incoming associations to this object.

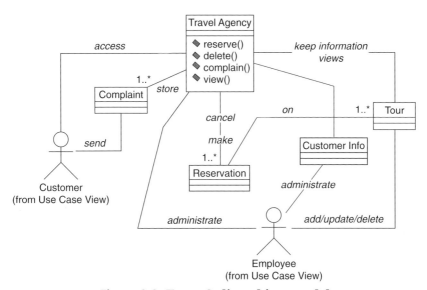

Figure 3-8. **Tours Online object model**

2.2.1 Derivation of the Object Model from the User Requirements

In what follows, we give the steps that lead to the initial object model in detail.

DETERMINING THE OBJECTS

The first step in determining the object model is finding the objects, like actors, that are mainly derived from names in the user requirements.

The list of names that we can deduce from the description of user requirements is shown in Table 3-3:

Travel agency	software
application software	users
information	employees
Reservation	**complaints** or suggestions
Complaint database	**employees**
Agency	facilities
operation information	people network
customers	**Tour**
tours	Agency
securities	agency
Employee	bureau
login ID	application
password	option
manager	client
Database	mail
Travel agency	

***Table 3-3.* Names in User Requirements**

The names that are marked through with a single line are not considered in the object model for the following reasons:

- Software, network, facilities, operation, and option: We consider theses names at this stage too general to be included in the object model.

- People, client, and users: Theses names all refer to the same name **customer**. We deleted these because they are redundant.

- Bureau: This name refers to the travel agency; it is redundant.

- Mail: There is no need to have an object to keep track of the mail. We might need it in a later stage either as an object or as an attribute.

- Securities: This is refined in terms of two attributes, login ID and password, which are marked in italic in Table 3-3 and are appropriate as attributes.

- Manager: The manager can be considered an employee of the travel agency, so there is no need to consider it as a separate object.

The names that are included as objects in the object model are retained for the following reasons:

1. **Travel agency:** we need to keep track of information on the travel agency because information is the core of the application.

2. **Tour:** This is a special class that stores all the information about tours.

3. **Reservation:** This class will be used for storing the exact information on tour reservations, including the cost incurred by the reservation.

4. **Complaints:** This class captures complaints to the agency made by customers.

5. **Customer:** This class holds data about the customer such as name, login ID, password, and credit card number.

6. **Employee:** This class captures attributes and behaviors of the employees, in particular, the behavior of validating the login ID and the password of a customer who wishes to login into the system and perform administrative tasks.

DETERMINING ASSOCIATIONS

The list of verb phrases that we can deduce from the description of user requirements is shown in Table 3-4.

The verb phrases with a line through them were eliminated for the following reasons:

- *"Software for a travel agency provides reservation facilities"*: This verb phrase is eliminated because "software" has been eliminated as an object (see determining the objects). "Reservation facilities" is another expression for operations on tours that are covered in other phrases.

- ~~Software for a travel agency provides reservation facilities.~~
- **People** wish to travel on tours **by accessing** a built-in network at the **agency bureau**.
- The **application** software **keeps information** on **tours**.
- **Users** can **access** the **system**.
- (**User**) **makes** a **reservation on** a **tour**.
- **Users** **view information** about the **tours** available without having to go through the trouble of asking the employees at the agency.
- The third option is to **cancel** a **reservation** that he/she made.
- Any **complaints** or suggestions that the **client** may have could be **sent** by e-mail.
- . . . to the **agency** or **stored** in a **complaint** database.
- The **employees** of the corresponding **agency** could use the application to **administrate** the system's operations.
- **Employees** could **add, delete, and update** the information on the customers and the **tours**.
- ~~he employee . . . to access the database of the travel agency.~~

Table 3-4. Verb phrases in user requirements

- *"the employee . . . access the database of the travel agency"*: This verb phrase only provides us with additional information for the need for a login ID and a password. In fact, employee "access" is covered by "update, delete, and add."

The remaining verb phrases represent explicit relations between every two objects in the object diagram.

Next we consider these verb phrases one by one:

1. *"**people** who wish to travel on tours **by accessing** a built-in network at the **agency bureau**"*

    "people" in the verb phrase is captured by the object name **customer** in our object model. The name "agency bureau" stands for the travel agency object. Hence, we have two object names **customer** and **travel agency** related by the verb expression "**by accessing**," which stands for an association between the two objects in the object model. This association is replaced by the verb **access**.

2. "The **application** software **keeps information** on **tours**."

    The name "application" refers to the travel agency object. Hence, we have two object names, **travel agency** and **tour**, related by the verb expression "**keeps information**," which stands for an association between the two objects in the object model because the travel agency stores and keeps information about the tours.

3. "***Users*** can ***access*** the ***system***."

   "Users" in the verb phrase is captured by the object name ***customer*** in our object model. The name "system" stands for the travel agency object. Hence, we have two object names, ***customer*** and ***travel agency***, related by the verb expression "**access**," which stands for an association between the two objects in the object model. This association was already identified in the verb phrase "people who wish to travel on tours by accessing a built-in network at the agency bureau."

4. "(***User***) **makes** a ***reservation*** **on** a ***tour***."

   The name "User" is an alternative for the object name ***customer*** in our object model. Hence, we have two object names, ***customer*** and ***reservation***, related by the verb "**make**," which stands for an association between the two objects in the object model. But since a customer should first go though certain phases before reserving in a tour, this association is no longer directly between the *customer* and the *reservation* objects but rather between the customer through ***travel agency*** and ***reservation***, which holds the data about the customer and the price to be paid. From this association arises a new one between the ***reservation*** and the ***tour*** object classes. This new association is expressed by the association "**on**" between the reservation and the tour because the reservation is made in a tour.

5. "To **view information** about the ***tours*** available without having to go through the trouble of asking the employees at the agency."

   Here we have two object names, ***travel agency*** (implicitly implied) and ***tour***, related by the verb expression "**view information**," which stands for an association between the two objects in the object model because the travel agency allows the customer to view information about the tour.

6. "The third option is to **cancel** a ***reservation*** that he/she made."

   Here we have two object names, ***travel agency*** (implicitly implied) and ***reservation***, related by the verb expression "**cancel**," which stands for an association between the two objects in the object model because the travel agency allows the customer to cancel a reservation.

7. "Any ***complaints*** or suggestions that the ***client*** may have could be **sent** by e-mail."

Here we have two object classes, **customer** and **complaint**, related by the association "**sent**" expressed by the verb "**send**."

8. "... to the **agency** or **stored** in a **complaint** database."

   Here we have two objects, **travel agency** and **complaint**, related by the association "**stored**." Note that an object "database" could have been introduced between "complaints" and "travel agency," but we preferred to postpone that because the term "database" is used to design the analysis phase.

9. "The **employees** of the corresponding **agency** could use the application to **administrate** the system's operations."

   Here we have two object classes, **employee** and **travel agency**, related by the association "**Administrate**."

10. "**Employees** could **add, delete, and update** the information on the customers and the **tours**."

    We have two object classes, **employee** and **tour**, related by the verb expression "**add, delete, and update**."

DETERMINING ATTRIBUTES

Now that the main associations have been determined, we are ready to find the attributes that can be deduced from the description or from general knowledge. Some attribute names appear in the description of the user requirement. Some others are added to express specific attributes about the objects.

FROM USER REQUIREMENTS

We identify two names that are valid as attributes. These are **ID** and **password**, which belong to the object class **employee**. Both of these allow employees to access the application and update the database. In addition, we add **name** as an attribute in class **employee**. For the class **customer**, we found, in the constraints related to the user requirements description, the need to have **loginID** and **password** attributes for the class **customer**.

The remaining attributes are determined from general knowledge analysis of the problem, as follows.

1. **Travel agency:** This object class is given a **name** and an **address** attribute.

2. **Customer:** This class is given **CustName** (*customer name*) and **CustID** (*customer ID*) attributes. The **CustID** attribute is important for distinguishing customers who have the same name.

3. **Tour:** This object holds the data about the tours. It is given two main attributes, the tour *Name* and the tour *Destination*. These are needed to maintain data on tours.

2.3 SOFTWARE SYSTEMS ARCHITECTURE (VERSION 1)

The architecture determines subsystems of our application. It can be derived, starting from the user requirement description, by trying to determine the main functions that our system needs to process. Additional subsystems can be derived from knowledge of the problem. Figure 3-9 presents an initial subsystem model that is derived based on user requirements.

The architecture of the project has been divided into five subsystems that interact with the user, on one hand, and with one another, on the other hand.

Derivation of the Subsystems from the User Requirements

The word "accessing" guides us to a subsystem responsible for accessing the system by all users. Such a system ensures access that occurs through a single secure path. In fact, the task of this subsystem is to ensure proper authorized access to all subsystems. We call this subsystem **System Access**.

The words "update," "delete," "add," and "stored" in the user requirements focus on managing the information stored in the database. It would

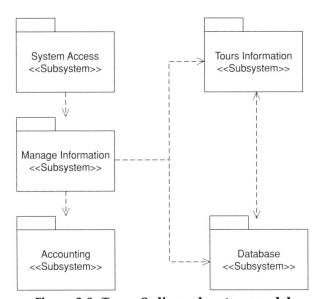

***Figure 3-9.* Tours Online subsystem model**

be more efficient to have a module responsible for the management of the information related to the tour so that we do not have to face problems when many people access the information and try to modify it simultaneously. Such a subsystem will be called **Manage Information**.

An additional subsystem that seems reasonable is one that is responsible for managing information on tours. This subsystem is implied by the phrase "view information," which stands for everything related to viewing the information related to the tour and data on tours. We shall refer to this subsystem as **Tours Information**.

An additional subsystem should be added that is responsible for all the transactions related to the payment process. In other words, this subsystem will be responsible for returning the price of the chosen trip to the customer, ensuring a secure path for the customer when paying by credit card, and making sure that the customer credit card is a valid one. Such a subsystem will be called **Accounting**.

Finally, we see that all the information about the customer and the tour information needs to be stored somewhere in our system. This means that we need to have a special subsystem responsible for handling this data. In fact we see in our description of the user requirements the word "database." This subsystem will be called **Database**.

Description 3-3 provides a glossary of these subsystems.

Glossary

1. ***System Access:*** responsible for all the travel agency access by the customer and by the employee of the travel agency.

2. ***Manage Information:*** is the subsystem responsible for all the reservations, canceling existing reservations, and record of all the complaints of the customers. It is also responsible for providing the information for the employees.

3. ***Accounting Subsystem:*** is responsible for all the accounting information; it performs checking and crediting of the current customer's account.

4. ***Tours Information:*** provides the information about the tours for the customers and stores the budget for each tour.

5. ***Database:*** is the subsystem that stores the information on tours that are stored by the travel agency for every tour. It also has the ID forms filled out by the customers.

Description 3-3. Tours Online subsystems description

Communication among Subsystems

The aforementioned subsystems communicate as follows.

At first, the customer communicates with the subsystem System Access. The Manage Information subsystem communicates with the subsystems Tours Information, Database, and Accounting. Moreover, the subsystem Manage Information communicates with the customers for reservation, cancellation, and complaint purposes. Finally, the Tours Information communicates with the subsystem Database from which it retrieves its information.

2.4 TRACEABILITY

In what follows, we carry two trace activities.

1. Use case to objects: This allows us to determine how use cases will be realized by objects of the object model.

2. Objects to architecture: this allows us to determine the contribution of an object to the architecture model.

Both trace activities are essential to bring the three models of a subsystem's architecture together, consequently ensuring validation of the subsystems at an early stage. Note that we do not explicitly trace through subsystems. This follows by the transitive relation shown here:

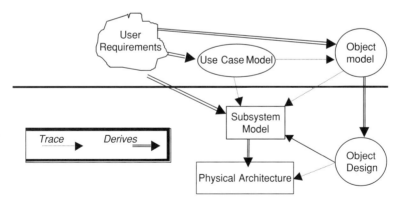

We expect to achieve the following advantages from the traceability:

1. Determine the objects that are owners of intermediate states of an activity diagram.

2. Determine the need and role of design objects that need to be added.

3. Determine new useful associations such as functions for objects.

4. Refine the analysis model to a more detailed design model.

Collectively, items 1–4 cooperate to ensure that a use case can be realized in an implementation.

2.4.1 Use Cases to Objects

Figures 3-10 to 3-15 give the result of tracing the activity diagrams in Figures 3-2 to 3-7, respectively, through the object model in Figure 3-8. The following is a key that determines the meaning of some notations in subsequent diagrams.

    ———→Communication in the same object class
    ———►Communication between distinct object classes related through
        an explicit association
  - - - - ►Communication between distinct object classes not related by
        an explicit association

---

1. FROM THE ACTIVITY DIAGRAM *STARTING* TO THE OBJECT MODEL

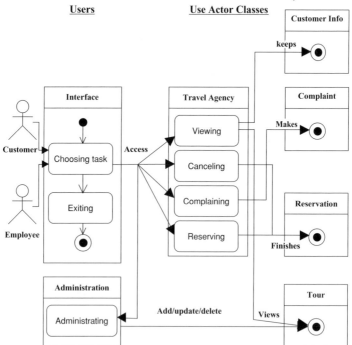

***Figure 3-10.* Trace of Starting activity from Figure 3-2**

Figure 3-10 shows the trace of Starting Activity in Figure 3-2 through the object model in Figure 3-8. Note that an interface class is introduced that provides a single entry and exit point for the functions of the system captured by class Travel Agency. Note also the appearance of classes Tour, Class Info and Reservation that were not explicitly present in Figure 3-2. Also a new class Administration has been introduced that support functionality required by an employee to manage the system.

The trace has reversed the role of customer and employees from external border access to internal objects bounded by the travel agency while providing the same required functionality. With this, an actor is left as a concept of a user, whereas the details of use are captured by corresponding use actor classes. The class "Customer Info" corresponds to the database class that stores the data related to the customers. It is worth noting how the final state of the activity is represented in terms of four different final states depending on the choice made by the user.

2. FROM THE ACTIVITY DIAGRAM *RESERVING* TO THE OBJECT MODEL

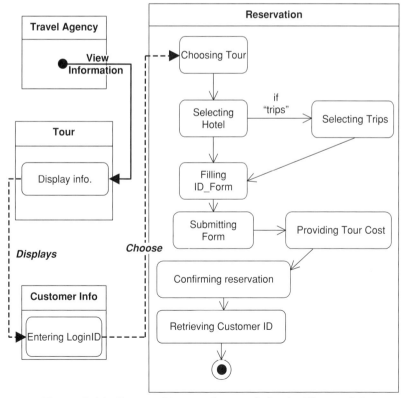

Figure 3-11. Trace of Reserving activity in Figure 3-3

Figure 3-11 shows the trace activity of the Reserving activity diagram in Figure 3-3 through the object model in Figure 3-8. The customer has to go through some specific steps in order to reserve in a tour. He should first access the travel agency, then view all the available tours, fill out a proper customer info form, and then reserve in the tour. The customer has to pass through four different phases, each of which is captured by a certain class. Hence, there is a need for additional relations, which are modeled by dashed arrows such as the relations between the "Tour" and the "Customer Info," and between the "Customer Info" and "Reservation." The newly added relations are captured as associations in a refined version of the object model in Figure 3-8.

3. FROM THE ACTIVITY DIAGRAM *VIEWING INFORMATION* TO THE OBJECT MODEL

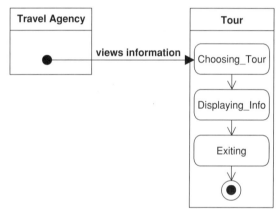

Figure 3-12. **Trace of Viewing Information activity in Figure 3-4**

Figure 3-12 shows the trace of the Viewing Information activity in Figure 3-4 through the object model in Figure 3-8. In order to view the information with respect to a certain tour, the employee or customer has to retrieve the data from the tour class.

4. FROM THE ACTIVITY DIAGRAM *CANCELING A RESERVATION* TO THE OBJECT MODEL

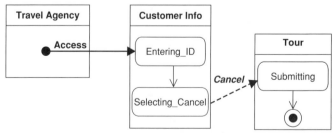

Figure 3-13. **Trace of Canceling activity in Figure 3-5**

Figure 3-13 shows the trace of the Canceling activity in Figure 3-5 through the object model in Figure 3-8. For security reasons, the customer has to provide the system with his login and password whenever he wants to cancel a tour reservation. Hence, he has to go through the "Customer Info" class first and then to the "Tour" class. Such a relation is identified in the initial object model. It is modeled by a – – – ▶ dashed arrow as a prospect association in the refined version of the object model in Figure 3-8.

5. FROM THE ACTIVITY DIAGRAM *ADMINISTRATE* TO THE OBJECT MODEL

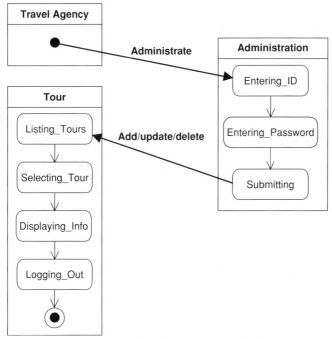

Figure 3-14. Trace of Administrate activity in Figure 3-6

Figure 3-14 shows the trace of the Administrate activity in Figure 3-6 through the object model in Figure 3-8. Whenever an employee wants to update the information about the tours, he has to provide the system with his login and password, which are to be validated in the class "Administration" that corresponds to the employees. Then the employee will update all the tour information stores in the class "Tour."

6. FROM THE ACTIVITY DIAGRAM *COMPLAINING* TO THE OBJECT MODEL

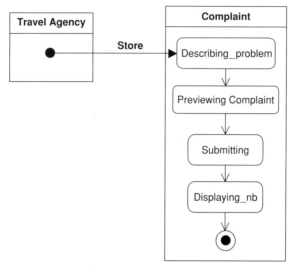

***Figure 3-15*. Trace of Complaining activity in Figure 3-7**

Figure 3-15 shows the trace of the Complaining activity in Figure 3-7 through the object model in Figure 3-8. In case a customer wants to send a complaint to the travel agency, he has to directly access the "Complaint" class, which is directly responsible for handling such situations. In fact, this class allows the customer to write a complaint and send it via e-mail.

Object Traceability Summary

This section provides a summary of the trace activities performed. Tables 3-5 through 3-10 show traced use case and corresponding objects, including clients and suppliers, as well as associations that correspond to transitions between states. The new associations between the objects were modeled previously using dark dashed arrows, and are displayed in bold and italic.

Use Cases to Objects

Note that the dashed lines in the trace diagram are capture newly added associations are denoted by bold and italics, similarly for newly introduced classes.

1. *STARTING* USE CASE

Step in Scenario	Association	Supplier Object	Client Object
Viewing	Access	Travel Agency	**Interface**
Canceling	Access	Travel Agency	**Interface**
Complaining	Access	Travel Agency	**Interface**
Reserving	Access	Travel Agency	**Interface**
Administrate	Access	**Administration**	Travel Agency
Exit viewing	Views	Tour	Travel Agency
Exit *administrating*	Add/Update/ Delete	Tour	**Administration**
Exit complaining	Makes	Complaint	Travel Agency
Exit canceling	Finishes	Reservation	Travel Agency
Exit reserving	Finishes	Reservation	Travel Agency

Table 3-5. **Mapping of "Starting" to associations in object model**

2. *RESERVE* USE CASE

Step in Scenario	Association	Supplier Object	Client Object
Displaying Info	View Info	Tour	Travel Agency
Entering Login ID	**Displays**	Customer Info	Tour
Choosing Tour	**Chooses**	Reservation	Customer Info

Table 3-6. **Mapping of "Reserve" to associations in object model**

3. *VIEW INFORMATION* USE CASE

Step in Scenario	Association	Supplier Object	Client Object
Choosing Tour	Views Info	Tour	Travel Agency

Table 3-7. **Mapping of "View Information" to associations in object model**

4. CANCEL USE CASE

Step in Scenario	Association	Supplier Object	Client Object
Entering ID	Access	Customer Info	Travel Agency
Submitting	*Cancel*	Tour	Customer Info

Table 3-8. Mapping of "Cancel" to associations in object model

5. ADMINISTRATE USE CASE

Step in Scenario	Association	Supplier Object	Client Object
Entering ID	Access	Administration	Travel Agency
Listing Tours	Add/Update/Delete	Tour	*Administration*

Table 3-9. Mapping of "Administrate" to associations in object model

6. COMPLAIN USE CASE

Step in Scenario	Association	Supplier Object	Client Object
Describing Problem	Store	Complaint	Travel Agency

Table 3-10. Mapping of "Complain" to associations in object model

2.4.2 Objects to Architecture

Object/Class Name	Subsystem Kind
Travel Agency	System Access Subsystem
Customer	System Access Subsystem
Employee	System Access Subsystem
	Manage Information Subsystem
Reservation	Manage Information Subsystem
	Accounting Subsystem
Customer Info	Database Subsystem
Tour	Tour Information Subsystem
Complaint	Database Subsystem

Table 3-11. Mapping of objects to architecture

Figure 3-16 shows in detail how an object from the initial object model maps to the architecture.

Figure 3-16 was derived from two main figures: the object model (Figure 3-8) and the subsystem model (Figure 3-9).

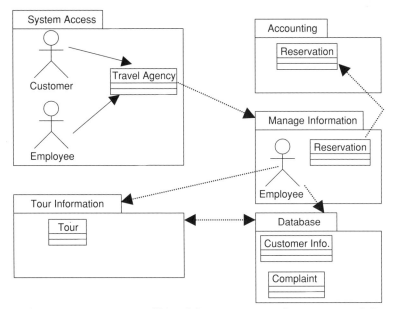

Figure 3-16. Tours Online object map to subsystem model

It is derived from the object model in that it relates the objects to the subsystems. For example, we have in the object model the class Customer associated with the class Travel Agency and the class Employee associated with the class Travel Agency.

It is also derived from the subsystem model because this diagram includes the relation among the subsystems of the architecture. For example, we have the subsystem System Access relating the class Travel Agency to the subsystem Manage Information, expressing the relation of the subsystem Access to the subsystem Manage Information in Figure 3-9.

The distribution of the classes on each of the subsystems was based on the subsystems' descriptions, which are displayed in Description 3-4 for ease of reference.

Glossary

1. *System Access:* is responsible for all the accessing of **travel agency** by the **customer** and by the **employee** from the travel agency.

2. *Manage Information:* is the subsystem responsible for all the **reservations**, canceling existing reservations, and recording all the complaints of the customers. It is also responsible for providing the information for the **employees**.

3. *Accounting:* is responsible for all the accounting information; it does the checking and crediting of the account of the current customer.

4. *Tours Information:* provides the information about the **tours** for the customers and stores the budget for each tour.

5. *Database:* stores the information on the tours that are stored by the travel agency for every tour. It will also have the **ID forms filled out by the customers**.

Description 3-4

When considering the description, what we notice, for example, is in the description of the *Access* subsystem the existence of the words "**Customer**," "**Employee**," and "**Travel Agency**," which were included in the *System Access* subsystem in Figure 3-16.

The description of the *Manage Information* subsystem includes the words "**Reservation**" and "**Employee**" and, hence, those corresponding classes were included in the *Manage Information* subsystem.

The *Accounting* subsystem is responsible for all the accounting information relevant to a customer. We know that this computation comes as a result of the customer reserving a tour or canceling a reservation. Hence, the related class "**Reservation**" was added to the *Accounting* subsystem. Having the class "**Reservation**" in the *Accounting* and the *Manage Information* subsystems means that it is part of both subsystems.

As for the *Tour Information* subsystem, it contains the word "**Tour**" and, hence, the class Tour was added to the *Tour Information* subsystem.

Finally, the description of the subsystem *Database* contains the expression "*ID forms filled out by the customer,*" which refers to the classes **Customer info** and **Complaint**.

3. CONSTRUCTION

This phase involves refinement of the analysis model to obtain a design model.

3.1 USE CASE (VERSION 2)

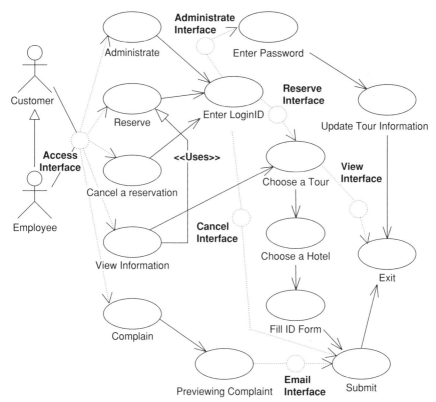

***Figure 3-17.* Tours Online use case model (version 2)**

The new use case model was derived from use case model version 1 (Figure 3-1), the activity diagrams (Figures 3-2 to 3-7), and the object map to architecture (Figure 3-16).

It is derived from the use case model (Figure 3-1) because it includes all of the main use cases of the first use case model.

It is also derived from the activity diagrams (Figures 3-1 to 3-7), because we took into consideration all the states in the activities diagram that refer to an action in the application and we added it as a use case in the use case model. Note that use cases should not be duplicated, even if it represents the same state in two or more different activity diagrams. An example of this appears in the use case "Enter Login ID," which is common to the use cases Administrate, Reserve, and Cancel activities diagrams. Since the state "Enter Login ID" was represented as a single use case, we had to include three interfaces, "**administrate interface**," "**reserve interface**," and "**cancel interface**" after the use case "Enter Login ID" in order to differentiate between the different paths to be followed after entering the login ID in each of the Canceling, Reserving, and Administrating cases. For the same reason, we had to add the interface "**view interface**" after the use case "Choose a Tour" to differentiate between the path to be chosen when reserving a tour and when viewing tour information. As for the "**e-mail interface**," it was added because the e-mail function is a completed interface that relates the application to other resources, such as the Internet and networks, and this should be handled by a special interface.

We also referred to the "object map to subsystem model" (Figure 3-16) because it helped us in generating the "**Access Interface**" between the actors (employee and customer) and the five use cases (administrate, cancel, reserve, view information, and complain). This interface was derived from the internal link between the travel agency class from one side and the employee and customer actors from the other side in the access subsystems.

In addition, we notice that the employee can act as a customer at any moment because an employee can also reserve a space for himself in a certain tour. Hence, we have an inheritance relationship between the employee and the customer. We also have a "**uses**" relationship between the two use cases "View Information" and "Reserve," because whenever a customer needs to make a reservation, he/she has to view the available tour information.

3.2 DYNAMIC MODELING (SEQUENCE AND COLLABORATION DIAGRAMS)

In this section we introduce sequence and collaboration diagrams that reveal the dynamic behavior of the system in terms of dynamic interaction among and within objects. Figures 3-18 to 3-29 give the sequence and collaboration diagrams for scenarios 3-1 to 3-5 respectively. Each scenario is given a sequence and a collaboration diagram.

Sequence and collaboration diagrams are useful as a basis for object design as well as method design. In general an outgoing message from a client to a supplier object would correspond to call of a method in the supplier by the client object. An incoming message, represented with a backward arrow captures the response of the supplier object to a method call. Consequently many useful methods and detailed interactions could be identified and derived from these diagrams.

1. A) STARTING SEQUENCE DIAGRAM

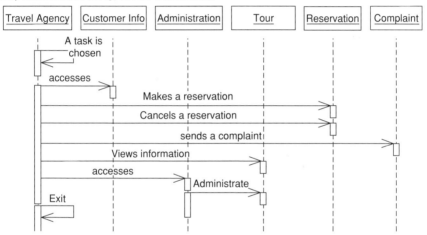

Figure 3-18. **Tours Online Starting sequence diagram**

B) STARTING COLLABORATION DIAGRAM

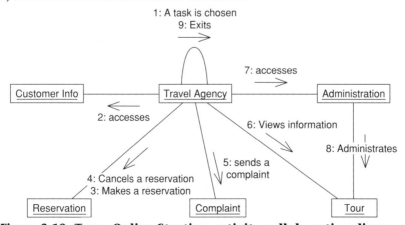

Figure 3-19. **Tours Online Starting activity collaboration diagram**

2. A) RESERVING SEQUENCE DIAGRAM

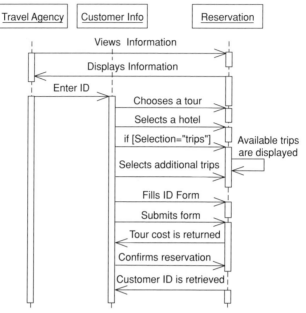

Figure 3-20. **Tours Online Reserving activity sequence diagram**

B) RESERVING COLLABORATION DIAGRAM

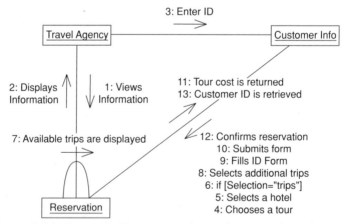

Figure 3-21. **Tours Online Reserving collaboration diagram**

3. A) VIEWING INFORMATION SEQUENCE DIAGRAM

Travel Agency
Tour
Wants to view information
Chooses a tour
Information about the tour is displayed
Customer exits

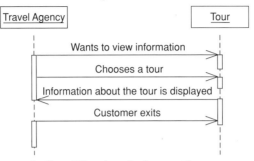

***Figure 3-22.* Tours Online Viewing Information sequence diagram**

B) VIEWING INFORMATION COLLABORATION DIAGRAM

1: Wants to view information
2: Chooses a tour
4: Customer exits
Travel Agency
Tour
3: Information about the tour is displayed

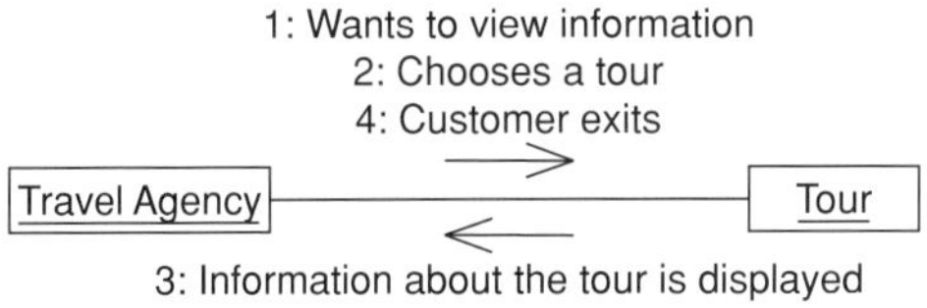

***Figure 3-23.* Tours Online Viewing Information collaboration diagram**

4. A) CANCELING A RESERVATION SEQUENCE DIAGRAM

Travel Agency
Customer Info
Tour
accesses
Enters his Login
if [Login ID="valid"] then customer selects the "Cancel" button
Customer submits the form
Customer exits

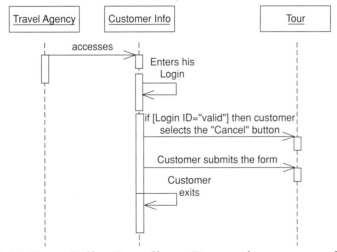

***Figure 3-24.* Tours Online Canceling a Reservation sequence diagram**

B) CANCELING A RESERVATION COLLABORATION DIAGRAM

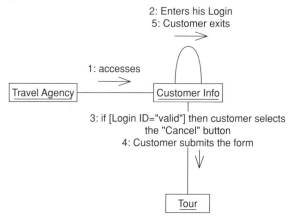

Figure 3-25. **Tours Online Canceling a Reservation collaboration diagram**

5. A) ADMINISTRATE SEQUENCE DIAGRAM

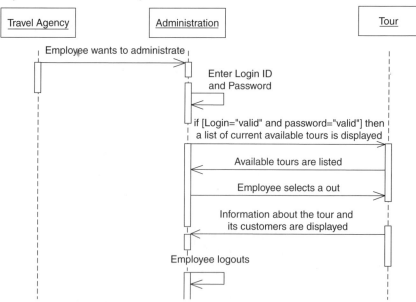

Figure 3-26. **Tours Online Administrate sequence diagram**

B) ADMINISTRATE COLLABORATION DIAGRAM

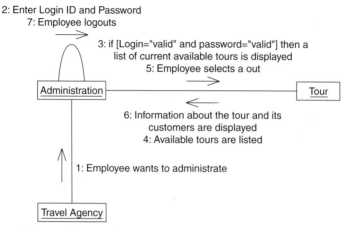

Figure 3-27. **Tours Online Administrate collaboration diagram**

6. A) REGISTERING A COMPLAINT SEQUENCE DIAGRAM

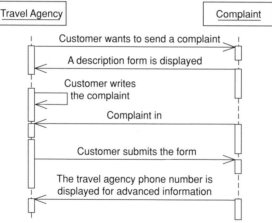

Figure 3-28. **Tours Online Registering a Complaint sequence diagram**

B) REGISTERING A COMPLAINT COLLABORATION DIAGRAM

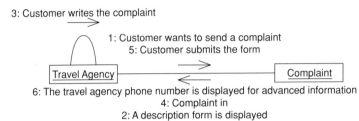

Figure 3-29. Tours Online Registering a Complaint collaboration diagram

3.3 OBJECT DESIGN

The object design in Figure 3-30 is a consequence of the preceding activities.

Derivation of the Object Design from the Object Model

Figure 3-30 has an object design model derived from the object analysis model in Figure 3-8.

The second version of the object design details the first version that was derived directly from user requirements.

In the following we clarify how the object design is obtained.

1. MULTIPLICITY IN THE OBJECT ANALYSIS MODEL THAT LEADS TO DATA STRUCTURE CLASSES

- ***ListOfEmpl, ListOfCust:*** Each added class is for a certain reason. First, we added the classes ***ListOfEmpl*** and ***ListOfCust*** and placed them between the Travel Agency class and the Employee class, and the **Travel Agency** class and **Customer** class, respectively. The point of adding these classes is to model data structures that would be implemented later on as an array, stack, or queue according to the programmer's desire. This type of added classes is needed to resemble a container; that is, ***ListOfEmpl*** and ***ListOfCust*** contains the list of the employees at the travel agency and the list of the customers of the agency, respectively.

2. FROM THE OBJECT MAP TO ARCHITECTURE (FIGURE 3-16)

- ***Starting_Page:*** The class ***Starting_Page*** was added for security reasons for checking the validity of both the customer login ID and the employee password. Similarly, the two functions ***Check_CustID*** and ***Check_EmpPass*** were added. The class ***Starting_Page*** was deduced

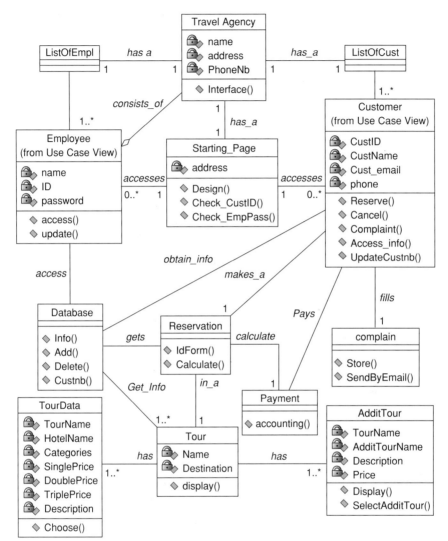

Figure 3-30. Tours Online object design model

from the existence of the subsystem *Subsystem Access* and was placed between the two classes **Customer** and **Employee** (Figure 3-16). It was also deduced from Figure 3-17, which expresses the interface **Access Interface** between the Employee and Customer from one side and any other class from the other side. This class also has a new function, ***Design***, in which the code for the design of this page would be implemented.

• ***Database:*** The class **Database** was derived from Figure 3-16. The main reason for adding such a class is that the class ***Tour*** holds a lot of information, so much that it is better to separate it into two classes. Hence the **Database** class will take care of all the information related to the customer reservations in a tour in terms of separation of functionality. In fact, from Figure 3-16, we notice that the *Subsystem Database* is related to the *Subsystem Tour Information*. Because the *Subsystem Tour Information* contains the class **Tour** in the new object design, the class **Database** becomes related to the class **Tour**. Also the *Subsystem Database* is related to the *Subsystem Manage Information*, and because the *Subsystem Manage Information* contains the two classes **Employee** and **Reservation**, then the class **Database** becomes related to the class **Employee** from one side and to the class **Reservation** from the other side.

- *Payment:* In Figure 3-16, we notice that the *Subsystem Manage Information* communicates with the *Subsystem Accounting*. We have in the *Subsystem Manage Information* the object class **Reservation**. Hence, the class **Payment** was designed as a class in the *Subsystem Accounting* to be responsible for the money aspect in the process of tour reservation. In our project, this mainly dealt with calculating the budget of the tour. Hence, a new function ***Accounting*** was added to the class **Payment** and an association **calculate** was added between this newly added class and the **Reservation** class. This new function is not responsible for calculating the price of the tour but rather for handling the payment process by credit card.

3. FROM USE CASE MODEL (VERSION 2)
- *Interface:* This function was added to the class **Travel Agency** as the result of the existing interface between the customer and employee from one side and each of the application tasks (such as cancel and reserve) from the other side.

4. NEW FUNCTIONS FROM TRACEABILITY DIAGRAMS
- *Reserve, Cancel, Complain, Access_info:* These functions were moved from the travel agency into the class **Customer**. This was a result of the trace activity in Figure 3-10. The states of "reserving," "canceling a reservation," "complaining," and "viewing information" were applicable to the customer and consequently they were transferred from the class **Travel Agency** to the class **Customer**.

- *Access, update:* These functions were added in the class **Employee** because, according to trace activity in Figure 3-10, the employee is the only one who "administrates" the database of the travel agency.

- *CustID, CustName, Cust_email, phone:* These attributes are added to class **Customer**. These are derived from trace activity in Figure 3-11, from "entering_ID" where the customer has to provide a personal ID and some extra information such as his/her name, e-mail address, and phone number.

- *ID, Name, password:* These attributes are added to class **Employee**. They are derived from the trace activity in Figure 3-14 because the employee has to "enter ID" and "enter password."

- *IdForm, Calculate:* These functions are deduced from states "fill ID form" and "providing tour cost" of the trace activity in Figure 3-11.

5. FROM MAPPING USE CASES TO ASSOCIATIONS IN OBJECT MODEL (TABLE 3-5)

- *Reservation:* This class already exists in the object model (version 1). In the refined model, it is repositioned between the two object classes **Customer** and **Tour**. The justification for this action can be depicted in Table 3-5, where a new association for every dashed trace was introduced. In Table 3-5 we have the two object classes **Customer** and **Reservation** related together by a newly defined association. This association models the heavy dashed arrow between the two classes. Hence, we had to relate the class **Reservation** to the class **Customer** from one side to remove the ambiguity and keep the class **Reservation** related to the class **Tour** from the other side because of the already existing relation.

- *Database:* We also have added a class **Database** between the two object classes **Customer** and **Tour**. The justification for this action is in Table 3-5, where a new association for every dashed trace was introduced. In Table 3-5 we have the two object classes **Customer** and **Tour** related together by a newly defined association. In fact, it turns out that the application has a lot of data to be kept somewhere for ease of the storing and managing information processes. We have also kept a record of the customer numbers in the **Database** class, through the function *Custnb*. Hence, the class **Customer** is associated with the class **Database**.

6. MORE KNOWLEDGE OF THE PROBLEM

- *UpdateCustnb:* The function *UpdateCustnb* is added to the class **Customer** to update the number of customers after each reservation. This was needed because we anticipated that there are limited reservations available in a tour, so this function was added to avoid an over-capacity problem.

- ***Sendbyemail: Sendbyemail*** is added to the class **Complain**, which is responsible for all complaints and suggestions from customers. We anticipate that this function will be needed to send complaints by e-mail.

- ***Customer info: Customer info*** is combined with class **Customer**, which is sufficient to take care of all the information related to the customers by itself.

- ***Tour Data:*** This class is responsible for handling the information about the hotels related to the selected tour, which is why it is related to the **Tour** object class. The reason for adding this class is that in each tour we have something like five to ten related hotels. If all the information about the tours and the hotels is to be stored and handled by one class, this will lower the speed of the application and make the information-browsing process slow.

- ***AdditTour:*** This class is responsible for storing the information about the additional trips related to a tour, which is why it is directly related to the **Tour** object class. The reason for adding this class is that in each tour we have something like five to ten related trips. If all the information about the tours and the trips is stored and handled by one class, this will lower the speed of the application and make the information-browsing process slow. Another reason is that the process of selecting the trips is optional; then it is easier to handle this process using a separate class alone then by using the **Tour** object class.

3.4 REVISITING THE SUBSYSTEM MODEL

Figure 3-31 represents the second version of the object design model map to architecture.

4. CONSTRUCTION/IMPLEMENTATION

The programming language for the implementation of Tours Online was chosen to be Visual J++ 6.0 because it is a prototype object-oriented programming language that provides an adequate environment for representing real-world objects. It is also user friendly by way of providing a graphical user interface, which helped in writing the code as easily as possible. It also helped in creating advanced graphical forms in a user-friendly interface.

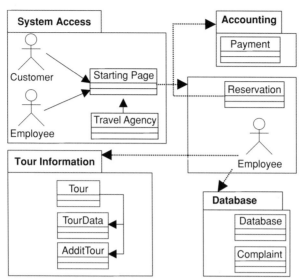

Figure 3-31. Tours Online object map to subsystem model (version 2)

The database was built in Microsoft Access 97. It was quite easy to store the customer and tour data in the database. MS Access 97 could be directly interfaced with MS Visual J++ 6.0, which justified its use.

The interfaces are classes implemented in Visual J++ 6.0. There is also the interface between the Java application and the database via a network.

The most interesting class was the "complaint" object class because it holds interesting Java library classes for sending e-mails through the network. The implementation heavily relied on the generic class forms because of using Visual J++.

4.1 INTERFACE OF MAIN CLASSES

Table 3-12 contains a summary of the design model (Figure 3-30) with some extra suggestion for implementation.

4.2 REVERSE ENGINEERING MODEL

Having completed all the design, a good way to discover if the design is compatible with the application is to generate the design model in reverse. In order to obtain such a result, we feed the application written in Java to the utility called GDPro, and we get the design model shown in Figure 3-32.

We notice that Figure 3-32 is quite different from the design model that we obtained in Figure 3-30. Note that the difference is not so big because we still

Class Name	Attributes	Functions	Remarks
Travel Agency	Name Address Phone	Interface();	
ListOfEmpl			Could be imple- mented using arrays.
ListOfCust			Could be imple- mented using arrays.
Starting page	Address	Design(); Check_CustID(); Check_EmpPass();	Here, by address, we mean URL address.
Employee	Name ID Password	Access(); Update();	
Customer	CustID CustName Cust_email Phone	Reserve(); Cancel(); Complain(); Access_info(); UpdateCustnb();	
Complain		Store(); Sendbyemail();	
Database		Info(); Add(); Delete(); Custnb();	
Reservation		IdForm(); Calculate();	
Payment		accounting	
Tour	Name Destination	Display();	
TourData	TourName HotelName Categories SinglePrice DoublePrice TriplePrice Description	Choose();	Choose could be elaborated in the implementation into choosing a hotel and making other choices.
AdditTour	TourName AdditTourName Description Price	Display(); SelectAdditTour();	Recall that select- ing a trip is op- tional and can be extented to more than one trip. This is handled by the functions.

***Table 3-12*. Summary of the design model**

have the object classes in Figure 3-32 identical to the object classes in Figure 3-30. The only difference arises in the existence of a new class called **Form** and the association between the class **Form** and each of the other classes. The reason for having such different associations is that the Form utility holds the major part of the programming – the Java application – hence, the GDPro software generated the new model in a way that the class **Form** is centralized among all the other classes, which was quite true in the implementation of the program. **Form** is a result of using J++.

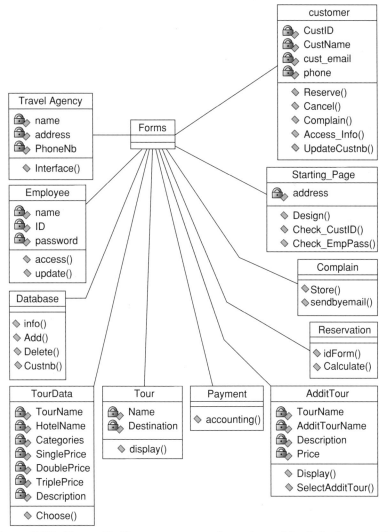

***Figure 3-32.* Tours Online reverse engineering object design model**

4.3 DEPLOYMENT AND PHYSICAL ARCHITECTURE

The software was designed so that it can run on any Windows platform, such as Windows NT Server, Windows NT Workstation, Windows 95, and Windows 98. Physically, the architecture could be identified as being a network-based **client–server** architecture with a **star topology.**

The software architecture was mapped to the physical architecture that we chose. In fact, if we go back to the final subsystem architecture for our application, we find it appropriate that these subsystems be physically grouped into two main subsystems. The first one is the **database subsystem** and the second one will group all the other subsystems. And as we can see, the **database subsystem** is the one we have on our server, whereas the group of the other subsystems is what we have on any other computer in the same network intranet area.

As we can see from the architecture that we arrived at, we have two main components: the first is the database and the second is the application itself.

ODBC is responsible for the administration of a data source, which is MS Access 97 in our case. In fact, ODBC should be configured in our example in every computer in which we install in it our application: the MS Visual J++ application.

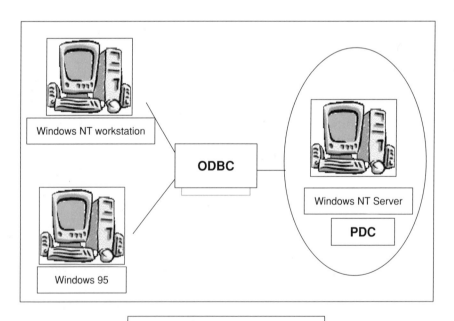

Figure 3-33. **Physical architecture**

The system was tested as an intranet network-based application. The database was ported on a Windows NT server so that any computer on the network could access it even if it is in a different domain. The application was ported on a computer with Windows NT workstation, Windows 95, or Windows 98. The only path for the interface between the application and the database is through the ODBC.

Chapter 4

Web Page Maker: Case Study 2

This chapter presents a case study on applying the bridge process for designing and developing an application for the Internet. The case study is special in the following sense: user requirements are a summary of information that the manager of an Internet service provider (ISP) provided to the developers. This resulted in requirements that include technical expressions including references to web page codes, fields, and specific interfaces. Nevertheless, with the bridge process we will find that it is possible to go through the design steps systematically and reach implementation while ensuring traceability among the use case, object, and architectural model.

1. INCEPTION

This phase opts to reach an expression of the user requirements in terms of a use case model.

1.1 USER REQUIREMENTS

User requirements are listed in Description 4-1.

Web Edit is a web page maker that allows any user who has a connection to the Internet and a web browser to use it to create a nice and simple web page. The project mainly consists of an interface that is a Java applet, which is loaded to the browser and connects to the web server, calls the right common gateway interface (CGI) script, and carries out one of its several functions.

The main aim of this project is to make the task of creating a web page as easy as possible and accessible by a wide range of users all over the world. To design and create a page by filling in some fields, a user has to provide some information. Note that the user does not require any knowledge of hypertext markup language (HTML) code or specific script language. Newly created pages can be saved on a server. This allows a user to preview a design page after creating it and before saving it on the web. In case he/she is dissatisfied with its design, the user can delete the web page at a later stage. The user can also upload the page at any time.

Description 4-1. Page Maker user requirements

1.2 USE CASE MODEL (VERSION 1)

Actors

For determining actors we will consider all the names then eliminate those names that do not stand for roles of users of the system. The elimination would also include multiple names that describe the same role. Names that describe roles of users most adequately are kept as described in the following.

~~Web Edit~~	~~web page maker~~	user	~~connection~~
~~Internet~~	~~web browser~~	~~web page~~	~~project~~
~~Interface~~	~~Java applet~~	~~browser~~	web server
~~CGI script~~	~~functions~~	~~project~~	~~task~~
~~Web page~~	users	~~page~~	~~fields~~
User	~~information~~	user	~~HTML code~~
~~Language~~	~~pages~~	server	user
~~Page~~	~~web~~	~~design~~	~~web page~~
User	~~page~~		

Table 4-1. List of names in user requirements

Table 4-1 shows all the names from user requirements that could possibly identify actors. All names in this table are eliminated except for **User** and

Server. We selected the word **User** because it represents any potential user of the application. The **user** actor has only to take care of choosing certain commands, but these commands cannot be translated and implemented on their own. That is why we should consider the **server** an actor because it will be the one responsible for running the corresponding programs for implementing the user requests. Hence, this actor stands as a virtual user of the system and its job is to execute and take care of the user commands. The words **web**, **page**, **browser**, **Internet**, **connection**, **HTML Code**, **Interface**, **Java applet**, and **CGI** were rejected because these only provide the technical meaning of the application. The words **Web Edit**, **project**, **functions**, **project**, **task**, **fields**, **information**, **Language**, and **design** are related to the design of the application.

Use Cases

Table 4-2 contains a list of all verb phrases of Description 4-1. Collecting these verbs is the first step toward determining use cases. Next all those phrases that are not associated with actors that were determined earlier are canceled out, which leaves potential use cases. The verbs kept in Table 4-2 are sufficient to model uses of the system as described in the following.

~~is~~	~~allows~~	~~has~~	~~to use~~
~~to create~~	~~consists~~	~~is~~	~~is loaded~~
~~connects~~	~~calls~~	~~carries out~~	~~is to make~~
~~To design~~	create	~~has to provide~~	~~saved~~
~~allows~~	to preview	~~is dissatisfied~~	can delete
upload			

Table 4-2. List of verbs in user requirements

The process of deriving the use cases is rather simple. In fact, let us take the verbs associated with the actor **User**. There are four main verbs associated with this actor: create, delete, upload, and preview. This leads us to derive four corresponding use cases: **Create Page**, **Delete Page**, **Upload Page**, and **Preview Home Page**. Now let us take into consideration the case of the **Server** actor. We already specified that the role of this actor is to execute the commands of the **User**. Hence, this actor is a recipient of the use case. The initial version of the use case model is displayed in Figure 4-1.

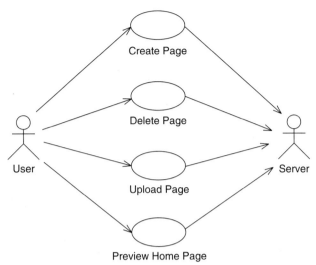

Figure 4-1. Page Maker use case model

Figure 4-1 shows an initial use case model composed of the resulting actors and cases. **User** and **Server** are the only actors. **User** captures the behavior of all possible users of the system. **User** and **Server** use cases are *Create Page, Delete Page, Upload Page,* and *Preview Home Page.*

Glossary

User: The user is the one who accesses the application and creates a home page. She/He can also delete it, upload it, and preview it.

Server: The server is responsible for running the corresponding programs for implementing the user requests. This actor stands as a virtual user of the system and its job is to execute and take care of the user commands.

Description 4-2. Page Maker glossary of actors

2. ELABORATION

This phase focuses on analyzing user requirements. This begins by documenting primary scenarios that could be determined from additional interviews with real system users. Primary scenarios are the preliminary step to determining activity diagrams and linking these to the use cases of the use case model obtained in the inception phase. In addition, the user requirements captured initially are analyzed to determine the initial object and component designs.

2.1 REQUIREMENTS ANALYSIS

This section presents the primary scenarios.

2.1.1 Primary Scenarios

The following scenarios are derived from discussion with the system owner on how the system will be used. Five primary scenarios are described. To focus this activity, use cases that were determined earlier set the stage for the necessary number of primary scenarios required. Each of the scenarios is given a name with pre- and postconditions that determine when a scenario may be activated and what conditions they will leave the target system in when the scenario finishes. The name of the activity diagram that will be derived from this scenario in the forthcoming sections is also indicated.

The scenario *Design Home Page* lists the steps the user performs in the process of designing a home page. The precondition ensures that the user is logged into the application. The postcondition asserts that the process terminates successfully when a home page is created (see Scenario 4-1).

1. NAME: DESIGN HOME PAGE (*ACTIVITY DIAGRAM 1*)

Precondition: Logged into Web Edit home page.
1. Visit our cool home page.
2. User chooses HTML editor called **WEB EDITOR**.
3. User starts a Free Page application.
4. User creates his/her own home page.
5. User previews his/her home page.
6. User saves his/her home page.
Postcondition: A home page is created.

Scenario 4-1

Scenario 4-2 lists the steps involved in the process of creating a home page. The steps include entering data, and choosing colors, banners, and other data relevant to creating a web page. The scenario requires that the "new page" option is chosen to begin the process. It terminates with a postcondition that requires that a page is created if the steps were performed successfully.

2. NAME: CREATE HOME PAGE (*ACTIVITY DIAGRAM 2*)

Precondition: User chooses "new page" option.
1. User enters a title for his design.
2. User has to enter – Heading.
                     – Heading font size.
                     – Heading color.
3. User chooses and checks the background color.
4. User enters information text.
5. User chooses the text color.
6. User also chooses the text style.
7. User inputs e-mail address.
8. User then chooses Java banner.
9. User also chooses banner text.
10. User chooses banner text color.
Postcondition: The home page has been created.

Scenario 4-2

The third scenario, *Preview Home Page,* lists the steps of the process of reviewing an existing page. The preview includes possible editing of the page followed by saving any changes that may have been entered. The postcondition requires that a page is previewed (Scenario 4-3).

3. NAME: PREVIEW HOME PAGE (*ACTIVITY DIAGRAM 3*)

Precondition: User page exists and user chooses "preview page" option.
1. User chooses the preview button and the editor sends the information to the server.
2. User previews page.
3. The editor enables the save option.
4. User saves page.
Postcondition: Page previewed.

Scenario 4-3

The *Upload Home Page* scenario (Scenario 4-4) describes the process of uploading an existing page. The last scenario, *Delete Home Page* (Scenario 4-5), describes the process of deleting a page. It requires a user to enter his/her password for authentication purposes. The postcondition ensures that the process terminates correctly when the page is deleted.

4. NAME: UPLOAD HOME PAGE (*ACTIVITY DIAGRAM 4*)

Precondition: User page exists and the user chooses the "upload" option.
1. User enters his/her user name.
2. User enters his/her password.
3. User uploads the page.
Postcondition: Page uploaded.

Scenario 4-4

5. NAME: DELETE HOME PAGE (*ACTIVITY DIAGRAM 5*)

Precondition: A home page exists and the user chooses option "delete page" on the editor applet application.
1. User signs a request ordered by the server and enters his/her user name.
2. User enters his/her password.
3. CGI search interface validates the user name and password.
4. The page is deleted and an info text file is returned as e-mail from the ISP assuring the page deletion.
Postcondition: The page is deleted.

Scenario 4-5

2.1.2 Secondary Scenarios

This section presents examples of possible secondary scenarios. Each secondary scenario is associated with one of the previously described primary scenarios.

Name: Connection Problems.
Primary Scenario: Design your home page.
The web browser fails to locate the site due to some protocol restrictions. The server might also be busy and the operation as a whole faces problems or is down due to some situation.

Name: Running Problems.
Primary Scenario: Create your home page.
The user does not conform to the rules of the application, which produces errors in the system.

Name: Interaction Problems.
Primary Scenario: Create your home page.
The server is unable to create a page because of some problems, such as inability to perform reads or writes on the server, using the CGI.

Name: Invalid Login and Password.
Primary Scenario: Delete your home page.
The server sends wrong identification data, preventing the continuity of the operations and causing the server to send a message to the user that navigation is denied, and the delete option is performed with mistakes shown in the message.

Other secondary scenarios may be added that may vary with security, robustness, and other similar nonfunctional requirements of the system.

2.1.3 Activity Diagrams
For every use case and corresponding scenario there is an activity diagram that shows the actions taken by the user to complete the process described in the scenario. To draw the activity diagrams, we follow the steps of primary scenarios. For each step we identify the phrase that would best describe an activity of the system that corresponds to this step. Each phrase is used to name a state in a corresponding activity diagram.

1. DESIGNING THE HOME PAGE ACTIVITY

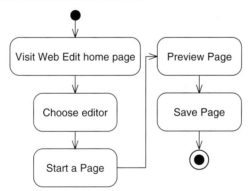

Figure 4-2. **Page Maker design home page**

Precondition: Logged into Web Edit home page.
1. **Visit our cool Home Page.**
2. User **Chooses html editor** called **WEB EDITOR.**
3. User **Starts a Free Page** application.
4. User **Creates his/her own home page.**
5. User **Previews his/her home page.**
6. User **Saves his/her home page.**
Postcondition: A home page is created.

For each step in the home page process we select the verb phrase that describes the activity in that step. A state is created for each of these steps. The states are joined in the same order presented in the scenario and initial and final states are added. Cumulatively, the aforementioned state activity diagram is obtained.

2. CREATING THE HOME PAGE ACTIVITY

Precondition: User chooses "new page" option.
1. User **enters a title** for his design.
2. User has to **enter** – **Heading.**
                       – **Heading font size.**
                       – **Heading color.**
3. User chooses and **checks the background color.**
4. User **enters information text.**
5. User **chooses the text Color.**
6. User also **chooses the text Style.**
7. User **inputs e-mail** address.
8. User then **chooses Java Banner.**
9. User also **chooses Banner Text.**
10. User **chooses Banner Text Color.**
Postcondition: The home page has been created.

Each of the states in Figure 4-3 corresponds to a step in the *Create Home Page* scenario.

3. PREVIEW THE HOME PAGE ACTIVITY

Precondition: User page exists and user chooses "preview page" option.
1. User **chooses the Preview Button** and the editor sends the information to the server.
2. User **previews page.**
3. The editor enables the **Save option.**
4. User **Saves page.**
Postcondition: Page previewed.

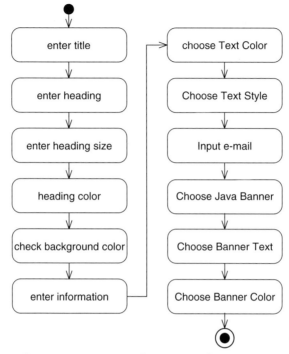

Figure 4-3. Page Maker create home page

Each state of the activity diagram in Figure 4-4 corresponds to one of the steps in the *Preview Home Page* scenario.

4. UPLOAD THE HOME PAGE ACTIVITY

Precondition: User page exists and user chooses the "upload" option.
1. User **enters his/her user name**.
2. User then **enters his/her password**.
3. User **uploads the page**.
Postcondition: Page uploaded.

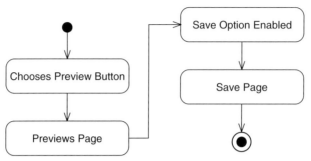

Figure 4-4. **Preview home page**

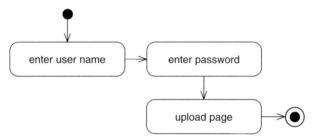

Figure 4-5. **Page Maker upload home page**

5. DELETE THE HOME PAGE ACTIVITY

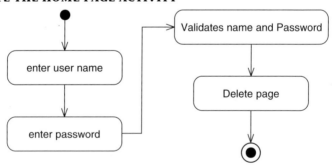

Figure 4-6. **Page Maker delete home page**

Precondition: A home page exists and the user is allowed to choose option "delete page" on the editor applet application.
1. The editor asks the user to sign a request ordered by the server and to **enter his/her user name**.
2. User has also to **enter his/her password**.
3. CGI search interface **validates user name and password**.
4. The **page is deleted** and an info text file is returned as e-mail from the ISP assuring the page deletion.
Postcondition: The page is deleted.

2.2 DOMAIN ANALYSIS: DERIVING THE INITIAL OBJECT MODEL

Figure 4-7 is an object model obtained from the user requirements in Description 4-1. Six objects are identified that correspond to names in the user requirements. By comparing Figures 4-1 and 4-7, note how the **User** and **Server** actors reappear as objects in the object model. Note as well how the use cases are modeled as functions in the main object of the application or as incoming associations to this object.

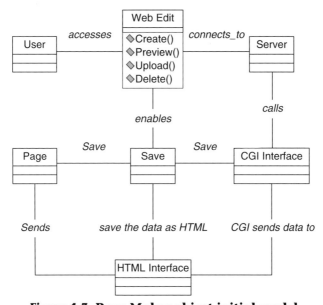

***Figure 4-7.* Page Maker object initial model**

Derivation of the Object Model from the User Requirements

In what follows, we give detailed steps that lead to the initial object model.

DETERMINING THE OBJECTS

In order to derive the classes for the object model, we have to take into consideration the names in the user requirements (Description 4-1) and retain only the valid ones. Table 4-3 contains all the names in the user requirements. Collecting these names is the first step in finding the objects. Next, only the names that are potential objects are kept; the remaining names are deleted.

~~page maker~~	**user**	~~connection~~	~~Internet~~
~~web page~~	~~project~~	~~interface~~	~~Java applets~~
~~applet~~	**web server**	**CGI**	~~functions~~
~~task~~	~~web page~~	~~users~~	~~world~~
~~fields~~	~~information~~	~~user~~	~~knowledge~~
~~server~~	~~user~~	~~designed page~~	~~web~~
~~web page~~	~~stage~~	~~feature~~	~~user~~
Web Edit	~~Web browser~~	~~Browser~~	~~Project~~
~~User~~	**HTML code**	~~Design~~	~~page~~

***Table 4-3*. Names in the user requirements**

Several reasons could lead to eliminating a name as a potential object. Redundancy is one reason. For example, all the names that are marked by a single line in Table 4-3 are considered redundant.

The words are not considered in the object model for the following reasons:

- "page maker," "connection," "Internet," "web browser," "web page," "project," "interface," "designed page," "applet," and "Java applets" are all related to the technical details; it is too early to consider these at this stage of the project.

- "task," "world," "functions," "fields," "information," "stage," "knowledge," "Project," and "feature" are very general and do not refer to anything specific and meaningful in this project.

The names that are in bold are those that are included as objects in the object model for the following reasons:

1. **Web Edit:** This is the main source for all the transactions performed by the user. In fact, in order to make a choice (delete, create, etc.) the user has to access this class and make a correct choice.

2. **Server:** For simplicity, "web server" was replaced by the term "server." The Web Edit class connects to the class server in order to display the application on the web. This class will be responsible for executing all of the user commands by interacting with the CGI and the chosen applications.

3. **CGI:** The CGI is an interface class responsible for establishing a connection between the server and the HTML. It was added for programming purposes because it is a major part of the application.

4. **User:** For managerial purposes the word "user" was replaced by a more specific term "user" since only the users who paid for the product can use it. The user is responsible for choosing from the Web Edit available services in order to design his/her page.

5. **Save:** Since neither the HTML, Server, nor the CGI classes were responsible for physically executing the saving process, a special class was added for this purpose. This class was added mainly because of the need for a special system responsible for storing the design data and a history of the user steps so that the data will not be lost. Hence, this class acts mainly as a database for the application.

6. **HTML interface:** This class is responsible for the HTML code behind the page design. In fact, this design is only done through HTML and so this consists of a major part of the application implementation. Therefore, we definitely need a class **HTML interface** to handle all the data sent by the CGI and to express it in a nice and coherent design.

Note: The main reason for having the three classes Server, CGI, and HTML interface at the analysis level is that they are at the core of the application. In other words, without theses three classes, a user will not be able to execute any of the described scenarios. These are designed as three different classes but each class has a totally different role in the application.

DETERMINING ASSOCIATIONS

For the associations between each of the object classes, we consider the verbs phrases associated with objects that were selected.

Table 4-4 shows a list of all verb phrases collected from the user requirements. Several of the verb phrases are not considered associations in the object

- Web Edit ~~is a web page maker.~~
- (***Web Edit***) **allows** any ***user*** who has a connection to the Internet.
- ~~Use it to create a nice and simple web page.~~
- ~~The project mainly consists of an interface.~~
- ~~(Interface) is loaded to the browser.~~
- ***This applet* connects** to the web ***server.***
- (***This applet***) **calls** the right ***CGI script.***
- ~~(This applet) carries out one of its several functions.~~
- ~~This project is to make the task of creating a web page as easy as possible.~~
- ~~To design and create a page by filling in some fields.~~
- ~~A user has to provide some information.~~
- ~~Note that the user does not require any knowledge of HTML code.~~
- Newly created pages **can be saved** on a ***server.***
- ~~This allows a user to preview his design page.~~
- ~~He/she is dissatisfied with his design.~~
- ~~He/she can delete the web page at a later stage.~~
- ~~The user can also upload his page at any time.~~

***Table 4-4.* Verb phrases in user requirements**

model for various reasons. In particular, the verb phrases with a line through them were eliminated for the following reasons:

- *"Web Edit is a web page maker"*: This verb phrase provides a general definition of Web Edit. Hence, we cannot deduce an association from this verb phrase. The verb used is "is," which suggests an inheritance relation that we overlook.

- *"Use it to create a nice and simple web page"*: This verb phrase explains more the usage of the function "create" in the application. Therefore, it does not provide any useful association.

- *"(Interface) is loaded to the browser," "The project mainly consists of an interface," and "(This applet) carries out one of its several functions"*: These verb phrases were eliminated because they do not contain any of the chosen classes.

- *"This project is to make the task of creating a web page as easy as possible" and "To design and create a page by filling in some fields"*: These phrases were eliminated because their meaning already appeared in the verb phrase "use it to create a nice and simple web page," where they all refer to the function "create."

- *"A user has to provide some information" and "Note that the user does not require any knowledge of HTML code"*: These verb phrases express two assumptions related to the application. The first one is that the user has to provide some information, and the second is that the user does not have to know HTML code. Hence, these assumptions only make things clearer and do not provide any new association.

- *"This allows a user to preview his/her design page"*: This verb phrase explains more the usage of the function "preview" in the application; therefore, it does not provides any useful association.

- *"He/she is dissatisfied with his/her design" and "He/she can delete the web page at a later stage"*: These verb phrases explain more the usage of the function "delete" in the application; therefore, they do not provide any useful association.

- *"The user can also upload his/her page at any time"*: This verb phrase explains more the usage of the function "upload" in the application; therefore, it does not provide any useful association.

The remaining verb phrases represent explicit relations between every two objects in the object diagram. We consider these verb phrases one by one, as follows.

1. "(**Web Edit**) **allows** any **user** who has a connection to the Internet"

   The name "User" stands for the object class User. Hence, the verb **allows** relates the **Web Edit** class and the **User** class. In fact, it expresses an association between these two classes because the user accesses the **Web Edit** class to perform some useful operations for his/her page design. A better verb to express this association would be **accesses**.

2. "**This applet connects** to the web **server**"

   The name phrase "this applet" stands for the object class Web Edit. Hence the verb **connects** relates the **Web Edit** class (expressed as "this applet") and the class **Server**. In fact, Web Edit connects to a server because in a web page application, the data are all stored in the server.

3. "(**This applet**) **calls** the right *CGI* **script**"

   The name phrase "this applet" stands for the object class Server because Server is the one able to communicate to the CGI and not the **Web**

Edit class. Hence, the verb "**Calls**" captures the association between the *Server* and the *CGI.* In fact, the Server calls the CGI to access the HTML interface.

4. "Newly created pages **can be saved** on a *server.*"

   The verb phrase **can be saved,** best expressed by the verb **save**, relates the *Server* and the *CGI* object classes. In fact, the CGI is responsible for saving any data that the server provides through it. Saving also occurs when the *HTML performed* some design action and needs to have it saved in order to have it published on the user web page later.

Two additional associations were derived out of knowledge of the problem domain.

5. *CGI sends data to:* The CGI is an intermediary between the server and the HTML interface. It redirects data from one to the other. Consequently, an explicit association between the CGI and the HTML interface is needed to capture this relation even if this association is not stated explicitly in the description. This explains why this is expressed as association in the object diagram.

6. *Enables:* This relates the *Web Edit* class and the *Save* class. In fact, the saving process is enabled indirectly by a user command. Because the user requests some functions to run in order to have a certain designed web page output, this acts as a motivator of the saving process and enables it.

Note: All of the associations were derived either from the user requirement description or from the classes description. The reason is that the user requirements and the classes were the only ones that clearly state the relation between each of the classes. In fact, because most of the classes were derived from the user requirements, it would be logical also to derive most of the associations from the verbs existing in the sentences where the two related classes are cited. But if the relation between a certain class pair was not clearly explained in the user requirements, then one should refer to the class descriptions and derive from it that relation.

DETERMINING ATTRIBUTES

Now that the main associations have been determined, we are ready to find the attributes that can de deduced from the description or from general knowledge. Some attributes are names that appear in the description of the user requirement part (Description 4-1). Others are added out of the use case model in order to express specific attributes about the objects.

FROM THE USE CASE MODEL

- **Create**, **Delete**, **Upload**, and **Preview**: In the use case model (Figure 4-1), we have four use cases: create, delete, upload, and preview home page. Since we are not yet sure about the complexity of these use cases, we added them as attributes in the class **Web Edit**. They might be considered later on as functions.

2.3 SOFTWARE SYSTEMS ARCHITECTURE (VERSION 1)

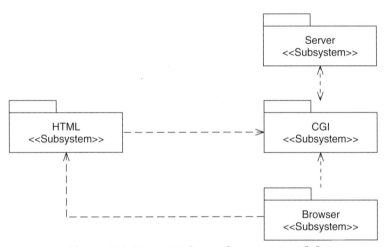

***Figure 4-8.* Page Maker subsystem model**

The architecture determines subsystems of our application. It could be derived starting from the user requirement description by trying to determine the main functions that our system needs to process.

Derivation of the Subsystems from the User Requirements

Looking into some of the words in the user requirements, we notice that we have the following words that suggest relevant subsystems:

Web browser, browser, web server, CGI script, HTML code, and server.

They were chosen for two main reasons. First, these terms are very specific in the sense that they can form specific subsystems, each with a different specific task. Second, these words hold a lot of variable meanings. For example, taking the word "web" into consideration, this could be related to the web design, to the web connection, to the Internet, and other meanings. So the role for the "web" subsystems involves performing many tasks. Therefore, a good way of identifying the subsystem is to take each name from the user requirements alone, write for it what connotations and ideas might be related to this name, and finally select the names that have the most relevant and important meanings in order to be considered subsystems.

Starting with "Web browser" and "browser," we notice that these state that the application is initialized from a closed system, which is the browser. In fact, the browser is the one that really browses the web, which is a collection of home pages uploaded to the remote system, the server. Hence, we introduce a subsystem called **Browser** to take care of this browsing task.

"Web Server" and "Server" denote the need of a **Server** subsystem to take care of the server main task, which is interacting with the CGI and taking care of the server/client function implied in any web application.

As for "HTML code," we notice that most of the design part in the application is done through HTML. Hence, we need to have a specific module responsible for such a tough task – we will call this subsystem **HTML**.

Finally, looking at the noun phrase "CGI script," we notice that the CGI relates any of the main already-selected subsystems "Browser," "Server," and "HTML" together. Therefore, it will mainly act as a subsystem interface and we will call this subsystem **CGI**.

Description 4-3 provides a glossary of the obtained subsystems.

Glossary

1. *Browser:* This is the application embedded in the HTML file, which stands as the main container of the applet application on the web. The browser consists of classes initializing the applet application on the server in its HTML container.

2. *Server:* This is a very basic application in the project process. It consists of the ordinary classes of the browser subsystem that interacts with the server through the CGIs.

3. *HTML:* This is not intended to mean HTML as a coding method, but it is meant to introduce the HTML as an interface as well as its capability to make a difference in its relation to the browser, which is absolute and can never be ignored.

4. *CGI:* This is a subsystem responsible for establishing a proper and correct relation between each of the HTML and Server, Server and Browser, and HTML and Browser.

Description 4-3. Page Maker subsystems description

Derivation of the Subsystems Relation from the Subsystems Description

From the description of the subsystems, we can determine which subsystem is directly related to the other.

Starting with the Browser subsystem, we can deduce from its description that it is directly related to the HTML interface, as stated clearly in its description: "application embedded in the HTML file."

For the Server subsystem, we can deduce that it is directly connected to the CGI: "through the CGIs."

For the HTML subsystem, it is clearly stated that it is directly connected to the browser subsystem: "relation to the browser."

As for the CGI subsystem, it acts mainly as an interface between each pair of subsystems. This is stated as such: "HTML and Server, Server and Browser, and HTML and Browser."

2.4 TRACEABILITY

This section determines traces of activity diagrams through the initial object model. A trace captures the flow of use cases when activated through objects. All dashed arrows correspond to new relations among objects and those will appear as associations in the design object model. Heavy arrows model relations that were already depicted. Light arrows are internal to objects.

2.4.1 Use Cases to Objects

1. FROM THE ACTIVITY DIAGRAM *DESIGN THE HOME PAGE* TO THE OBJECT MODEL

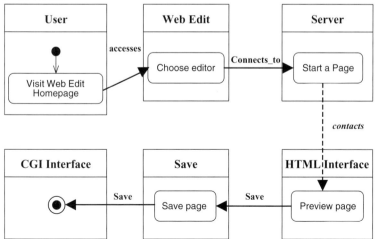

***Figure 4-9.* Page Maker trace of Design Home Page activity in Figure 4-2**

Note that the trace represents one activity of the system. Figure 4-1 captures the behavior of the system and the participation of objects in the object model when the design scenario is executed. The boxes resemble objects; the states within objects indicate that it is the responsibility of the object to execute the behavior in that state. Mapping states to objects needs to be guided by the responsibilities of the objects that were determined in the initial object design. For instance, visiting a page is triggered by the user, whereas "Chooses editor" is an edit activity; this is why it is mapped to the Web Edit object. On the other hand, it is the responsibility of the server to start a page; this explains why the state Start a Page is mapped to the server. Preview Page is mapped to the HTML Interface. The dashed arrow between Server and HTML Object is to indicate that the initial object model does not have a direct association between these two objects. The remaining arrows are solid to emphasize that additional direct associations to the existing ones between corresponding objects exist.

2. FROM THE ACTIVITY DIAGRAM CREATE THE HOME PAGE TO THE OBJECT MODEL

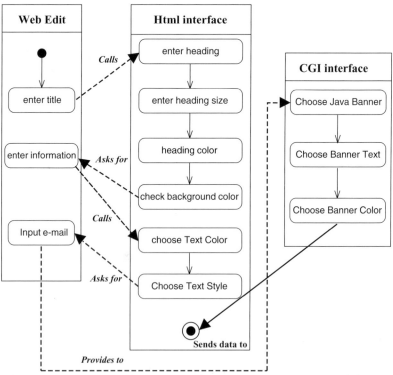

Figure 4-10. Page Maker trace of Create Home Page activity in Figure 4-3

The activity diagram in Figure 4-3 is mapped to three objects only. Note that the mapping resulted in many new direct associations among the objects that did not exist before.

3. FROM ACTIVITY DIAGRAM PREVIEW THE HOME PAGE TO THE OBJECT MODEL

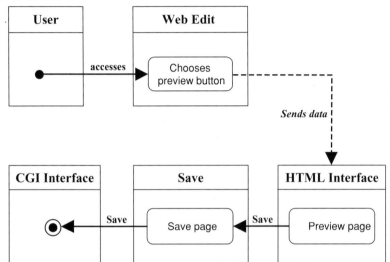

Figure 4-11. Page Maker trace of Preview Home Page activity in Figure 4-4

The activity diagram in Figure 4-4 is mapped to five objects as presented in Figure 4-11. The activity is triggered by object User and terminates in a CGI.

4. FROM ACTIVITY DIAGRAM UPLOAD THE HOME PAGE TO THE OBJECT MODEL

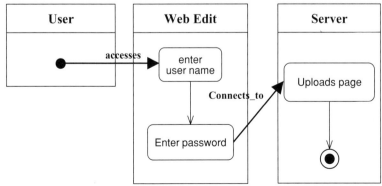

Figure 4-12. Page Maker trace of Upload Home Page activity in Figure 4-5

**5. FROM ACTIVITY DIAGRAM DELETE THE HOME PAGE TO THE OBJECT
MODEL**

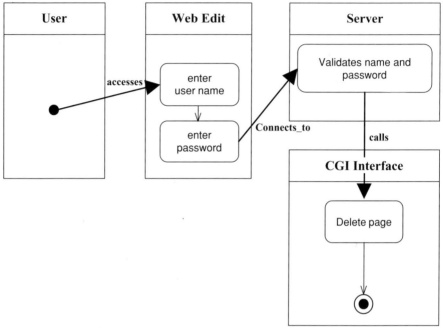

***Figure 4-13.* Page Maker trace Delete Home Page activity in Figure 4-6**

Traceability Summary

This section provides a summary of the trace activity performed from scenarios and activity diagrams to the object Model. Tables 4-5 to 4-9 show, for a given use case and its corresponding scenario, case steps in the scenario, the resulting or correspondind association and the objects, including clients and suppliers. New associations resulting from the trace activity are highlighted in bold and italics.

Use Cases to Objects

The dashed lines in the trace diagram are modeled by newly added associations that are denoted by bold and italics.

1. *DESIGN* USE CASE

Step in Scenario	Association	Supplier Object	Client Object
Choose HTML editor	Accesses	Web Edit	User
Start a Free Page	Connects_to	Server	Web Edit
Preview Home Page	**Contacts**	HTML interface	Server
Save Home Page	Save	Save	HTML interface
Exit Design	Save	CGI	Save

Table 4-5. Mapping of "Design" to associations in object model

2. *CREATE* USE CASE

Step in Scenario	Association	Supplier Object	Client Object
Enter heading	**Calls**	HTML Interface	Web Edit
Enter information	**Asks for**	Web Edit	HTML Interface
Choose text color	**Calls**	HTML interface	Web Edit
Input e-mail	**Asks for**	Web Edit	HTML interface
Choose Java banner	**Provides to**	CGI	Web Edit
Exit Create	Sends	HTML Interface	CGI

Table 4-6. Mapping of "Create" to associations in object model

3. *PREVIEW* USE CASE

Step in Scenario	Association	Supplier Object	Client Object
Choose Preview button	Accesses	Web Edit	User
Previews page	**Sends data**	CGI	Web Edit

Table 4-7. Mapping of "Preview" to associations in object model

4. *UPLOAD* USE CASE

Step in Scenario	Association	Supplier Object	Client Object
Enter user name	Accesses	Web Edit	User
Uploads page	Connects to	Server	Web Edit

***Table 4-8.* Mapping of "Upload" to associations in object model**

5. *DELETE* USE CASE

Step in Scenario	Association	Supplier Object	Client Object
Enter user name	Accesses	Web Edit	User
Validates name and password	Connects to	Server	Web Edit
Delete page	Calls	CGI	Server

***Table 4-9.* Mapping of "Delete" to associations in object model**

2.4.2 Objects to Architecture

Object/Class Name	Subsystem Kind
User	Server Subsystem
Web Edit	Server Subsystem
Server	Server Subsystem
CGI	CGI Subsystem
Save	Browser Subsystem
	Server Subsystem
HTML Interface	HTML Subsystem

***Table 4-10.* Mapping of objects to architecture**

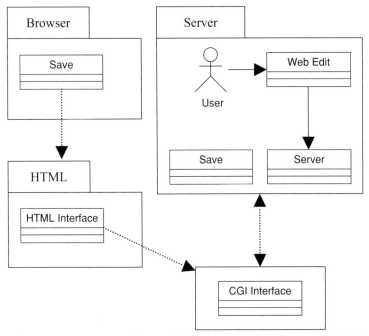

Figure 4-14. Page Maker object map to subsystem model

Mapping objects to architecture (Table 4-10) directs the division of responsibility among the subsystems. This helps to determine interfaces for subsystems and to narrow the communication interface.

Figure 4-14 shows in detail how the object maps to the architecture.

Figure 4-14 was derived from two main figures: the object model (Figure 4-7) and subsystem model (Figure 4-8).

It is derived from the object model because it relates the objects to the subsystems. It is also derived from the subsystem model because this diagram includes the relation between the subsystems of the architecture. In fact, we have the class Server, which is representative of the subsystem Server. We have the **CGI** class, which is related to the *subsystem CGI* in our architecture. We also have the **HTML interface** class, which is an indicator of the *HTML subsystem*. Finally, we have the class **Save**, which is related indirectly to the *Browser subsystem* because the *Browser subsystem* is the one responsible for saving the work. As for the relation between the subsystems, it is clearly stated in the associations between each of the stated classes in the object model.

In fact we have an association between the **Server** and the **CGI**, which is present in the subsystems architecture (Figure 4-8). We also have the association between the **Save** class and the **CGI**, which is representative of the relation between the ***Browser subsystem*** and the ***CGI subsystem***. We also have the association between the **Save** and **HTML interface** classes, which are related to the relation between the **Browser interface** and the **HTML interface**. Finally, we have the association between the **HTML interface** and the **CGI**, which is representative of the relation between the ***HTML subsystem*** and the ***CGI subsystem*** in our architecture.

The distribution of the classes between each of the subsystems was based on the subsystems description. The description is displayed in Description 4-4 for ease of reference.

Glossary

1. *Browser:* This stands for the application embedded in the HTML file, which stands as the main container of the applet application on the web. The browser really consists of classes initializing the applet application on the server in its HTML container.

2. *Server:* This stands for a very basic application in the project process. It consists of the **ordinary classes** of the browser subsystem that interact with the server through the CGIs.

3. *HTML:* It is not intended to mean **HTML** as a coding method, but it is meant to introduce the HTML as an interface as well as its capability to make a difference in its relation with the browser, which is absolute and cannot be ignored.

4. *CGI:* This is a subsystem responsible for establishing a proper and correct relation between each of the HTML and Server, Server and Browser, and HTML and Browser.

Description 4-4

Considering the description, we notice that the subsystems HTML, CGI, and Server are related to classes in the object model (Figure 4-7) with the same names. In other words, we have in the object model the class **Server**, which is related to the ***Server Subsystem***; the class **CGI**, which is related to the ***CGI Subsystem;*** and also the class **HTML**, which is related to the ***HTML Subsystem***. As for the subsystem Browser, we know that it is responsible for saving the data; hence, we relate the class **Save** to the ***Browser Subsystem***. We also notice that the ***Server Subsystem*** consists of ordinary classes, **User** and **Web Edit**. And since this subsystem is also responsible for backing up the data, we add to it the class **Save**.

3. CONSTRUCTION

This phase is concerned with refining deliverables, the analysis model to obtain a design model.

3.1 USE CASE (VERSION 2)

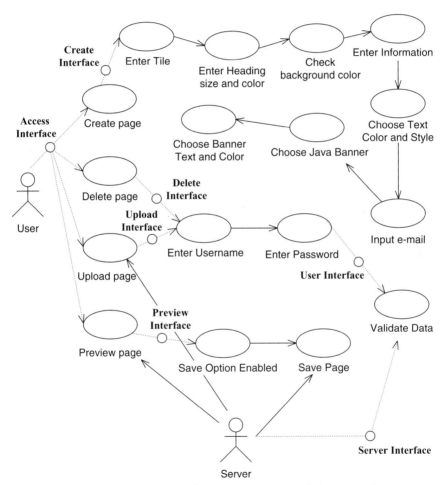

Figure 4-15. Page Maker use case model (version 2)

The new use case model was derived from the initial use case model, version 1 (Figure 4-1), and the activity diagrams (Figures 4-2 to 4-6) and object map to architecture (Figure 4-14).

The initial use case model is used as a basis. Then it is fleshed out with state activity diagrams. Each state in the activity diagram that refers to an action in the application is added as a use case to build version 2 of the use case model. In carrying this activity we make sure not to duplicate the use case even if it represents the same state in two or more different activity diagrams. An example of this appears in the use case "enter user name," which appears as a common state in each of the Delete and Upload activity diagrams. The state "enter user name" is represented as a single use case, and two interfaces, **Delete Interface** and **Upload Interface**, are added before the use case "enter user name" to differentiate between the way the system will deal with the entering user name options for each of deleting and uploading. Similarly, the interfaces **User Interface** and **Server Interface** are inserted before the "validate" use case to differentiate between how the actors user and server deal with this use case. Also, the interfaces **Preview Interface** and **Create Interface** are inserted before the state Save, which is common to the "create" and "preview" activity diagrams. As for the **Access Interface**, it is added to provide security when users access the application.

3.2 DYNAMIC MODELING: SEQUENCE AND COLLABORATION DIAGRAMS

In what follows, we present sequence and collaboration diagrams that capture the dynamic behavior of objects in the system. Each diagram corresponds to a scenario. The sequence diagram highlights the roles of objects in carrying the scenario and shows the progress of each with time. Collaboration diagrams also focus and highlight only the interactions among objects. Both of these could lead to new associations and functions in the object model and objects entities.

1. A) DESIGN THE HOME PAGE SEQUENCE DIAGRAM

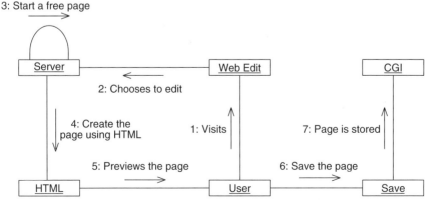

Figure 4-16. **Tours Online design home page sequence diagram**

This diagram shows the dynamic interaction of the five objects that would be involved in executing the scenario *Design Home Page*. The activity starts when the user object chooses to visit the Web editor, which triggers the message "edit" to the server, followed by designing a page and the server response to permit the user to review the design before the page is finally saved by the CGI object.

B) DESIGN THE HOME PAGE COLLABORATION DIAGRAM

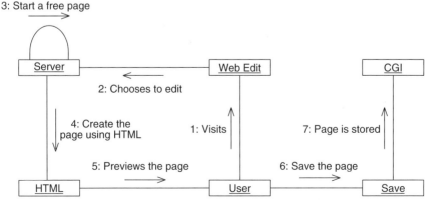

Figure 4-17. **Design the Home Page collaboration diagram**

2. A) CREATE THE HOME PAGE SEQUENCE DIAGRAM

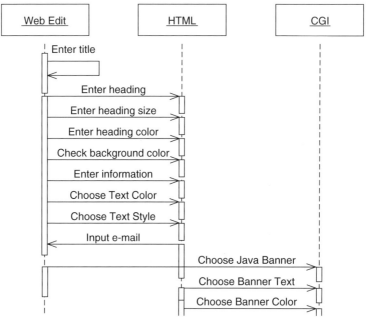

***Figure 4-18.* Page Maker Create the Home Page sequence diagram**

B) CREATE THE HOME PAGE COLLABORATION DIAGRAM

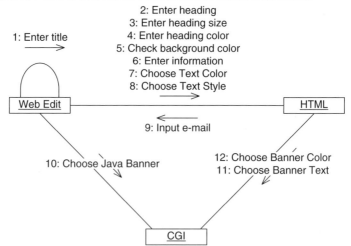

***Figure 4-19.* Page Maker Create the Home Page collaboration diagram**

3. A) PREVIEW THE HOME PAGE SEQUENCE DIAGRAM

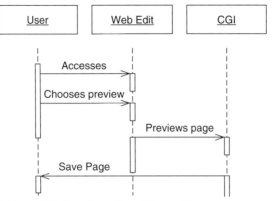

Figure 4-20. Page Maker Preview Home Page sequence diagram

B) PREVIEW THE HOME PAGE COLLABORATION DIAGRAM

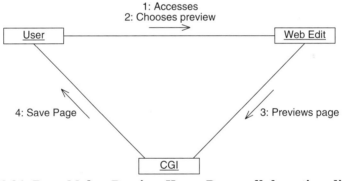

Figure 4-21. Page Maker Preview Home Page collaboration diagram

4. A) UPLOAD THE HOME PAGE SEQUENCE DIAGRAM

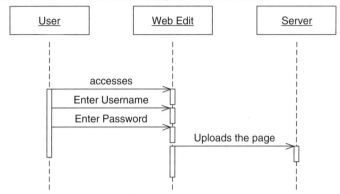

***Figure 4-22*. Page Maker Upload Home Page sequence diagram**

B) UPLOAD THE HOME PAGE COLLABORATION DIAGRAM

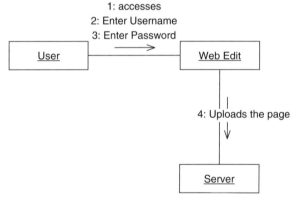

***Figure 4-23*. Page Maker Upload Home Page collaboration diagram**

5. A) DELETE THE HOME PAGE SEQUENCE DIAGRAM

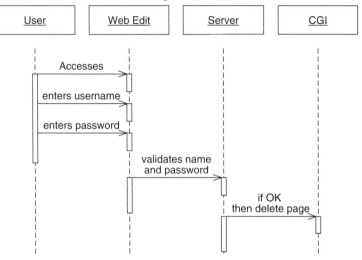

***Figure 4-24.* Page Maker Delete Home Page sequence diagram**

B) DELETE THE HOME PAGE COLLABORATION DIAGRAM

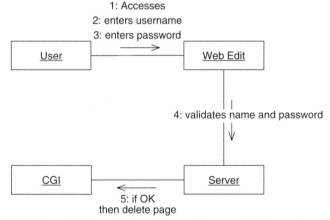

***Figure 4-25.* Page Maker Delete Home Page collaboration diagram**

3.3 OBJECT DESIGN

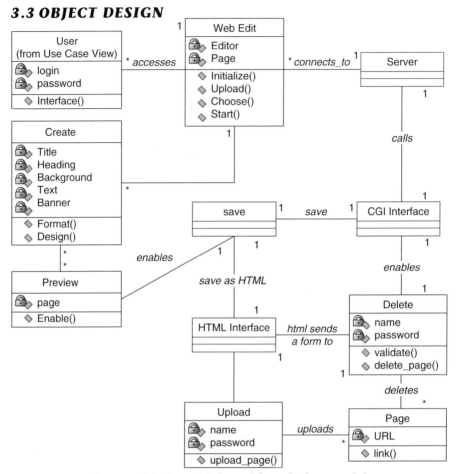

***Figure 4-26.* Page Maker object design model**

Derivation of the Object Design from the Object Model

Figure 4-26 shows version 2 of the object model, which is a detailed version of the object model in Figure 4-27. If we look at both object models, we notice that they are similar in the sense that most of the objects in the initial object model reappear in Figure 4-26.

Considering the second object model, we notice that some associations are kept between the following:

1. User and Web Edit classes

2. Web Edit and Server classes

3. Server and CGI classes

4. Save and CGI classes

5. Save and HTML interface classes.

We also notice that we had to add some classes, such as **Create**, **Preview**, **Upload**, and **Delete**.

In fact, if we go back to the first object model, we notice that these classes were actually functions in the *Web Edit* class. The reason was that we were not very sure of the complexity of these functions.

The object design was obtained based on the following.

1. FROM USE CASE MODEL (VERSION 2)

- *Delete:* The user enables the deletion process whenever he/she decides to delete the web-designed page. But the truth is that the process of the deletion is not completed directly by the user; instead, it is derived through a direct interaction between the HTML interface and the CGI. Because the web page is stored in the CGI, it is the responsibility of the HTML interface to interact with the CGI and physically delete the web page. This is why the ***Delete*** class was sitting between the HTML interface and the CGI.

- *Upload:* After creating the page, the user has to upload the web page on the web and give it a URL address so that it will be accessible and active.

2. FROM THE OBJECT MAP TO ARCHITECTURE (FIGURE 4-14)

- ***Interface***: This function was added in the class **User** as the result of the existing interface between the user and several functions in the class **Web Edit** to preserve the security of the application.

3. FROM MAPPING USE CASE TO ASSOCIATION IN OBJECT MODEL (TABLES 4-5 TO 4-9)

- ***Create:*** This class was a function inside the class **Web Edit**. We had to delete the function create from **Web Edit**, make a class ***Create***, and relate **Web Edit** directly through a new association *enables* to the class ***Create***.

   The reason for this direct association is depicted in Tables 4-5 to 4-9, which introduced a new association for every dashed trace. Hence, the user accesses the class **Web Edit** to create a class. So the main function of **Web Edit** is to enable the class ***Create*** so that the creation of the class will begin.

- **Preview:** This class was created as a result of the dashed line in Tables 4-5 to 4-9 in the delete scenario. In fact, logically one cannot preview a class that is not created yet; it was then logical to relate the class **Preview** to the class **Create** instead of the class **Web Edit**. Another association, related to the class **Preview**, is the one to the class **Save**. The reason is that after having created the page and previewed it, the user will be asked to save his/her new web page, which is why the class **Save** was directly related to the class **Preview**.

4. MORE KNOWLEDGE OF THE PROBLEM

- **Login, Password:** Some interesting attributes added to the class user were **Login** and **Password,** since before performing any critical action such as deleting a web page, the user will be asked to provide his/her login and password for security reasons.

- **Initialize**: For the class **Web Edit**, a new function was added, **Initialize**, since before starting to create his/her page the user will be asked to provide some useful information for security reasons.

3.4 REVISITING SUBSYSTEM MODEL

Figure 4-27 represents the second version of the object map to architecture. As we can see, we have added a new subsystem **System Access** as a result of the use case (Version 2; Figure 4-15). This subsystem is related to the user access to the **Web Edit** class. We added the two classes **User** and **Web Edit** in the system access subsystem.

For the **Server Subsystem**, we have removed the class **Save** because, according to the design model (Figure 4-26), it is not directly related to the class **Server**. But, at the same time, we have added the two classes **Create** and **Preview**, because there is an indirect relation between each of the subsystems **System Access** and **Server** through the class **Web Edit**. The class **Delete** was added to the subsystem **CGI** because the CGI is the one responsible for the deletion process, having appeared in the trace of the delete activity diagram (Figure 4-13).

4. CONSTRUCTION/IMPLEMENTATION

Visual J++ 6.0 was chosen as the programming language for the implementation for Web Edit. The client–server interface was handled by the **CGI driver,** which led to **CGI scripts** written in **PERL**. Table 4-11 gives a summary of the design classes.

Class Name	Attributes	Functions	Remarks
User	Login Password	Interface();	
Web Edit		Initialize(); Upload();	
Create			These classes contain all the Java commands related to page creation.
Preview			
Delete			
Server			
Save			
CGI			
HTML			
Interface			

Table 4-11. **Summary of the design model**

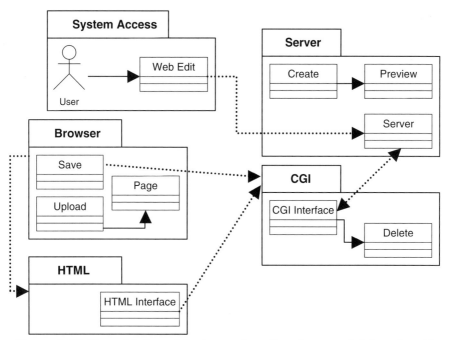

Figure 4-27. **Page Maker object map to subsystem model (version 2)**

Part III

AS IS Case Studies

This part introduces three case studies taken from different problem domains. The first case study is on simulation, the second is on education, and the third on product distribution. Each could be used as a model to build applications in similar domain by applying the Bridge process. The case studies present models reached leaving out the details of deriving these models as exercises to the reader. Each chapter concludes with exercises that guide the reader in this direction.

Chapter 5

Simulating a Robot Arm: Case Study 3

This case study is about simulating a mechanical robot arm. The design model is obtained as a consequence of applying the bridge process. Similar applications on simulation could be designed in a similar fashion. The user requirements are complemented up front by a glossary of terms, each of which denotes a component of the robot arm, the target of the simulation. In addition a picture is displayed to further clarify the concept. Note that the use case model is simple. It focuses on three activities; two of which, help and test, could be generalized to any application. The third focuses on the core activity of the application. In this sense the initial use case model is a good start to design and later build the application. The scenarios include describing help and test facilities that the application offer. The object model expresses aggregation and inheritance relations, showing how commonalties could be factored out to reach more concise models.

UML by Example

The chapter leaves out the details of derivation to give to the reader the opportunity to apply the bridge process and check the results against the models that are presented. The exercises at the end of the chapter guide the reader in this direction

1. INCEPTION

1.1 USER REQUIREMENTS

Description 5-1 gives a summary of the user requirements, and Description 5-2 lists a glossary of terms.

> The robot is designed to help move cars from one place to a truck. The arm has the following parts: a base sweeper, shoulder sweeper, elbow extension, arm extension, and gripper. An application will be designed to receive information about the object that is to be lifted. The object can either be a car or a block of metal. Should it be a car, the robot arm will automatically activate a gripper. If the object is a black of metal, the robot arm activates a motor that controls an iron rope. The user should start controlling the robot after the application has ensured that it is able to lift the object. The user can rotate the base sweeper, extend the elbow, or minimize or maximize the shoulder until the head of the arm reaches the top of the object. Then the user can press finish, which informs the robot arm to take control. The simulation of the robot arm will be manifested in the following actions.
>
> The application verifies that the robot is in the right position. Afterward, the base sweeper automatically rotates, the arm extends to full length, and the shoulder slides down to the height of the truck. The operating tool is turned off and the arm releases the object. The truck moves away and the arm returns to its original position. Note, however, that the user's attempt to move the object may fail or succeed.

Description 5-1. Robot arm user requirements

Glossary: *Definition of Some Technical Words*

Robot arm: This is a machine that consists of the base sweeper, extension parts, motor, and magnetic gripper. It transports lifted objects and controls both the electromagnetic current and the motor.

Junk car: This is one of the objects that can be selected to be lifted. It has a specific height and weight.

Base sweeper: This is the base of the robot arm. It is cylindrical in order to rotate, which leads to the rotation of the whole construct. It is connected to the shoulder extension. It can also move forward and backward.

Compressed object: This is one of the objects that can be selected to be lifted. It has a specific height, width, and type.

Elbow extension: This is part of the robot arm. It is connected to both the shoulder extension and the arm extension.

Shoulder extension: This is a part of the robot arm. It is connected to both the elbow extension and the base sweeper. It is defined as an extension part. It slides up and down, but there is a minimum and maximum height for the slide.

Arm extension: This is part of the robot arm. It is connected to both the elbow extension and the magnetic gripper. It is defined as an extension part. It slides forward and backward, but there is a minimum and maximum distance for the slide.

Rope: This represents a tool for lifting. It is connected to the motor and is controlled by the robot arm.

Motor: This is a part of the robot arm. It is connected to the arm extension and a rope. It is responsible for controlling the length of the rope.

Magnetic gripper: This is part of the robot arm. It is connected to the arm extension. Whenever the electromagnetic current is on, the gripper holds a car.

***Description 5-2.* Robot Arm Glossary of Technical Terms**

Picture Representing the Robot Arm

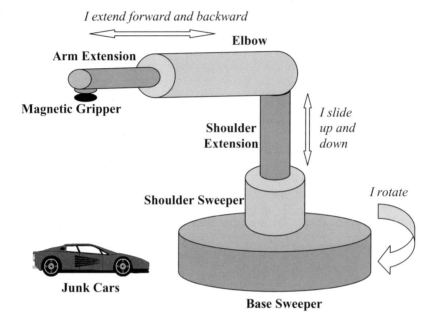

Such a diagram helps to clarify user requirements and simplifies the analysis process.

1.2 USE CASE MODEL (VERSION 1)

Figure 5-1 shows an initial use case model composed of one actor and three cases.

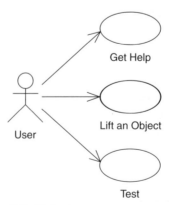

Figure 5-1. **Robot arm use case model**

User is the only actor that captures the behavior of all possible users of the system, including employees and managers. The user can perform one of the three actions: get help from the system, ask the robot to lift an object, and test the system using a demo module.

Both *Test* and *Help* use cases could be generalized to other applications. *Lift an Object* is the core of this simulation application. We expect that some aspects of the forthcoming analysis of this case could be generalized.

2. ELABORATION

2.1 REQUIREMENTS ANALYSIS

Analyzing requirements is done in terms of primary scenarios, secondary scenarios, and activity diagrams. The three lead to expansion of the use case model into a more elaborate model.

2.1.1 Primary Scenarios

In what follows, three different scenarios (Scenario 5-1, 5-2, and 5-3) are presented that detail the user cases. The *GetHelp* scenario describes the help facility of the system that guides the user during the application. The *LiftObject* scenario captures the bulk of the application. It describes how the different components of the robot arm could be manipulated to lift an object. The *Test* scenario describes how the user could test the functionality of the system.

It might be worth noting that activity number 5 of Scenarios 5-1 and 5-3 could be expanded with activities 6 through 14 of scenario 5-2. This suggests one common subscenario for primary Scenarios 5-1 and 5-2. We leave restructuring the scenarios and any consequences on the use case model and object design as an exercise to the user.

1. NAME: GET HELP *(ACTIVITY DIAGRAM 1)*

Precondition: The user wants the system to help him.
1. The user logs in the application.
2. The user chooses the "help" button.
3. The system plays music.
4. The system opens the help form.
5. The user learns how to use the application.
6. The help session ends.
7. The user returns to the main menu.
Postcondition: The user finished using the help.

Scenario 5-1

2. NAME: LIFT AN OBJECT *(ACTIVITY DIAGRAM 2)*

Precondition: The user wants the robot arm to lift an object.
1. The user enters the data about the object.
2. The system analyzes the data.
3. The system selects the proper tools in the robot arm to lift the object.
4. The user uses the "forward" and "backward" buttons to move the base sweeper to a better position.
5. The user uses the "down" and "up" buttons to slide the shoulder extension down or up just above the object.
6. The user uses the "extend" and "restrain" buttons to extend or restrain the arm extension into the proper position.
7. The user uses the "rotate left" and "rotate right" buttons to fix the position of the base sweeper to the right or left.
8. The user asks the robot arm to lift the object once the robot arm is in the correct position.
9. The user presses on the "release" button.
10. The base sweeper rotates by 90 degrees.
11. The arm extension moves forward.
12. The shoulder extension moves downward.
13. The robot arm releases the object at the target position.
14. The robot arm returns to its initial state.
Postcondition: The user finished lifting the object.

Scenario 5-2

3. NAME: TEST *(ACTIVITY DIAGRAM 3)*

Precondition: The user wants to test the system.
1. The user logs into the application.
2. The user chooses the "Demo" button.
3. The system plays music.
4. The system opens the demo form.
5. The user virtually manipulates the robot arm.
6. The test session ends.
7. The user returns to the main menu.
Postcondition: The user finished testing the system.

Scenario 5-3

2.1.2 Secondary Scenarios

Name: Mechanical Problems.
Primary Scenario: Lift an Object.
The user was not able to lift the object because the robot arm had a mechanical problem, such as the shoulder sweeper not being properly connected to the base sweeper.

Name: Energy Problems.
Primary Scenario: Lift an Object.
The robot arm electricity and battery energy are not full.

Name: Running Problems.
Primary Scenario: Get Help, Test.
The application is not running properly.

Activity Diagrams

1. GET HELP ACTIVITY

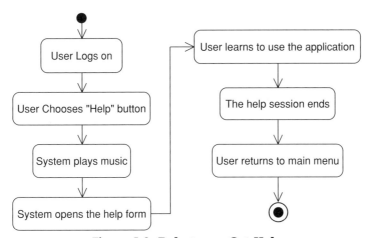

***Figure 5-2.* Robot arm Get Help**

Precondition: The user wants the system to help him.
1. The **user logs** in the application.
2. The **user chooses the "help" button**.
3. The **system plays music**.
4. The **system opens the help form**.
5. The **user learns how to use the application**.
6. The **help session ends**.
7. The **user returns to the main menu**.
Postcondition: The user finished using the help.

2. LIFT AN OBJECT ACTIVITY

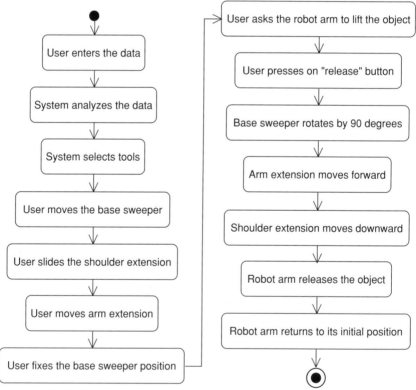

Figure 5-3. **Robot arm Lift an Object**

Precondition: The user wants the robot arm to lift an object.
1. The **user enters the data** about the object.
2. The **system analyzes the data**.
3. The **system selects** the proper **tools** in the robot arm to lift the object.
4. The **user** uses the "forward" and "backward" buttons to **move the base sweeper** to a better position.
5. The **user** uses the "down" and "up" buttons to **slide the shoulder extension** down or up just above the object.
6. The **user** uses the "extend" and "restrain" buttons to **extend or restrain the arm extension** into the proper position.
7. The **user** uses the "rotate left" and "rotate right" buttons **to fix the position of the base sweeper** to the right or left.
8. The **user asks the robot arm to lift the object** once the robot arm is in the correct position.
9. The **user presses on the "release" button**.
10. The **base sweeper rotates by 90 degrees**.
11. The **arm extension moves forward**.
12. The **shoulder extension moves downward**.
13. The **robot arm releases the object** at the target position.
14. The **robot arm returns to its initial state**.

Postcondition: The user finished lifting the object.

3. TEST ACTIVITY

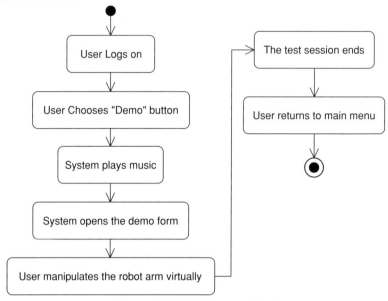

***Figure 5-4.* Robot arm Test**

Precondition: The user wants to test the system.
1. The **user logs** into the application.
2. The **user chooses the "Demo" button**.
3. The **system plays music.**
4. The **system opens the demo form.**
5. The **user virtually manipulates the robot arm.**
6. The **test session ends.**
7. The **user returns to the main menu.**
Postcondition: The user finished testing the system.

2.2 DOMAIN ANALYSIS: DERIVING THE INITIAL OBJECT MODEL

The object model in Figure 5-5 relies on aggregation and inheritance. The robot arm is modeled in terms of its components: *Elbow Extension, Base Sweeper,* and *Extension Parts.* All are connected to *Shoulder Extension,* which is

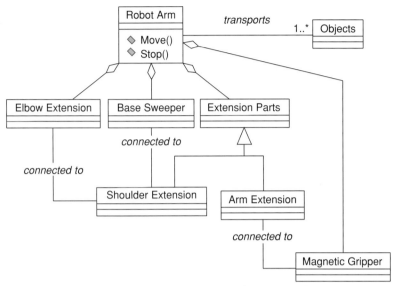

Figure 5-5. **Robot arm object model**

a descendant of *Extension Parts*. Class *Object* in the model denotes all possible kinds of objects that the robot can lift.

2.2.1 Derivation of the Object Model from the User Requirements

Objects are collected from the user requirements presented in Description 5-1. All names are potential objects. Only those names that best represent objects are kept; the rest are deleted. Similarly, all verb phrases in Description 5-1 are potential associations between objects. Only those associations that are related to selected objects are kept. The resulting objects and associations are linked together to form the object model in Figure 5-5.

DETERMINING THE OBJECTS

From the user requirements and the project description, we have chosen the following objects from the potential names (Table 5-1).

Robot	Base Sweeper	Extension Parts
Elbow extension	Object	Gripper
Shoulder extension		

Table 5-1. **Objects in user requirements**

2.3 SOFTWARE SYSTEMS ARCHITECTURE (VERSION 1)

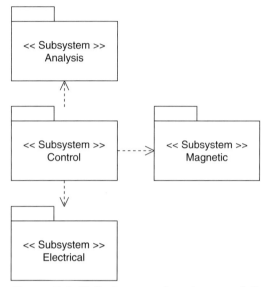

***Figure 5-6.* Robot arm subsystem model**

The architecture of the application has been divided into four subsystems that interact with each other. Description 5-3 provides a glossary of the obtained subsystems.

Glossary

1. ***Control:*** This is responsible for all the commands entered by the user to manipulate the robot arm.

2. ***Analysis:*** This is the subsystem responsible for analyzing the information related to the objects. It will decide whether the object is to be lifted or not.

3. ***Electrical:*** This is responsible for all the electricity that feeds the robot arm.

4. ***Magnetic:*** This subsystem is responsible for controlling the power of the magnetic gripper of the robot arm.

***Description 5-3.* Robot arm subsystems description**

Derivation of the Subsystems Relation from the Subsystems Description

The aforementioned subsystems communicate in the following way. The subsystem **Control** takes the result of the **Analysis** subsystem. Then, the **Control** subsystem communicates with the **Electrical** and the **Magnetic** subsystem to make sure that the lifting process is being done effectively.

2.4 TRACEABILITY

Traceability Summary

2.4.1 Objects to Architecture

Table 5-2 gives a summary of trace objects determined previously in the selected subsystems.

Object/Class Name	Subsystem Kind
Robot Arm	Analysis Subsystem
	Control Subsystem
Base Sweeper	Control Subsystem
	Electrical Subsystem
Extension Parts	Control Subsystem
	Electrical Subsystem
Elbow Extension	Control Subsystem
	Electrical Subsystem
Shoulder Extension	Control Subsystem
	Electrical Subsystem
Arm Extension	Control Subsystem
	Electrical Subsystem
Magnetic Gripper	Control Subsystem
	Electrical Subsystem
Object	Analysis Subsystem

Table 5-2. **Mapping of objects to architecture**

3. CONSTRUCTION

3.1 USE CASE (VERSION 2)

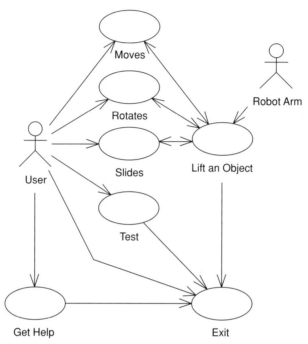

***Figure 5-7.* Robot arm use case model (version 2)**

This use case model (Figure 5-7) introduces new use cases ***Moves***, ***Rotates***, ***Slides***, and ***Exit***. The use cases ***Moves***, ***Rotates***, and ***Slides*** are derived from activities of primary Scenario 5-2 described earlier and could be viewed as subcases of the *LiftObject*, *Help*, and *Test* use cases. The *Exit* use case gives one exit point for all activities of the user. In addition, Figure 5-7 introduces a new actor, ***Robot Arm***, which represents the robot and optimizes the interaction between several functions.

3.2 DYNAMIC MODELING: SEQUENCE AND COLLABORATION DIAGRAMS

1. A) GET HELP SEQUENCE DIAGRAM

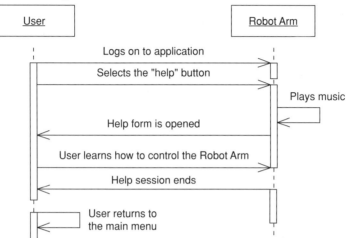

Figure 5-8. Robot arm Get Help sequence diagram

B) GET HELP COLLABORATION DIAGRAM

7: User returns to the main menu   3: Plays music

1: Logs on to application
2: Selects the "help" button
5: User learns how to control the Robot Arm

User   Robot Arm

6: Help session ends
4: Help form is opened

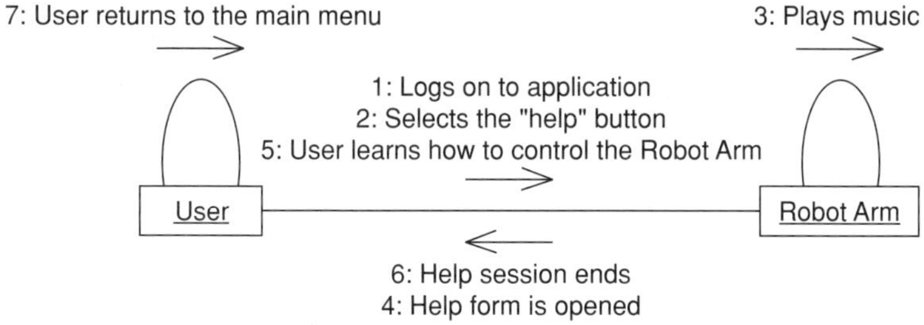

Figure 5-9. Robot arm Get Help collaboration diagram

2. A) LIFT AN OBJECT SEQUENCE DIAGRAM

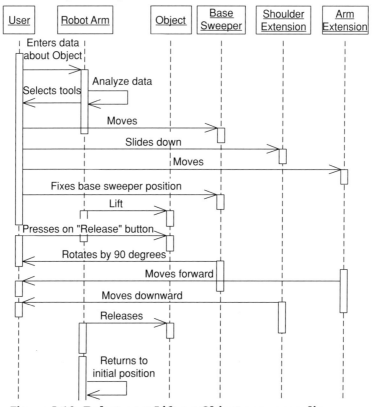

***Figure 5-10.* Robot arm Lift an Object sequence diagram**

B) LIFT AN OBJECT COLLABORATION DIAGRAM

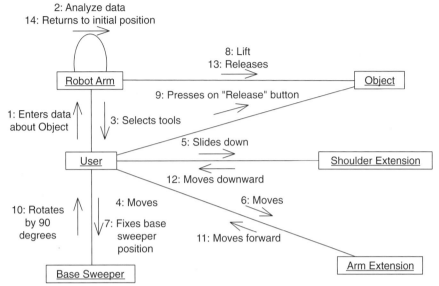

Figure 5-11. **Robot arm Lift an Object collaboration diagram**

3. A) TEST SEQUENCE DIAGRAM

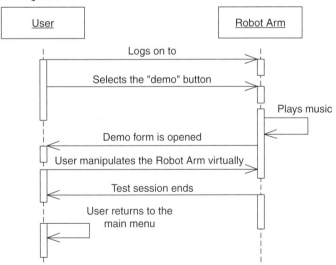

Figure 5-12. **Robot arm Test sequence diagram**

B) TEST COLLABORATION DIAGRAM

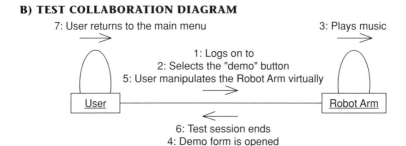

Figure 5-13. **Robot arm Test collaboration diagram**

3.3 OBJECT DESIGN

The object design details the initial object model. Most of the classes are taken from the initial object model that describes the several parts in the robot arm. This explains the aggregation relationship between the "Robot Arm" class and other classes. The functions such as "Rotate," "Move," and "Lift" were derived from the use case model (Figure 5-7). Classes *Rope, Motor,* and *Magnetic Current* are implementation classes that capture actual details of how the simulation will be implemented. Class *Object* of the initial object model is substituted for by classes *Lifted Object* and two descendants that capture specific objects that are to be lifted. Class *Lifted Object* denotes the database that holds the information, either the junk cars or the compressed object. The inheritance relation allows for extending the application to permit the robot arm to lift objects other than the one specified by the descendant classes.

4. CONSTRUCTION/IMPLEMENTATION

Figure 5-15 gives the object model obtained by reverse engineering of one implementation in Delphi 2.0. OpenGL, Corel Draw, 3dstudio, and 3dimpact were also used in building the application.

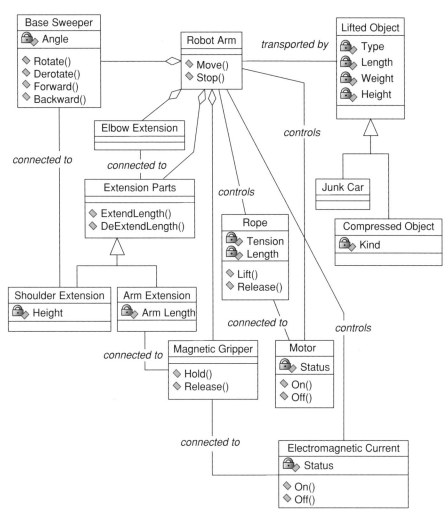

***Figure 5-14.* Robot arm object design model**

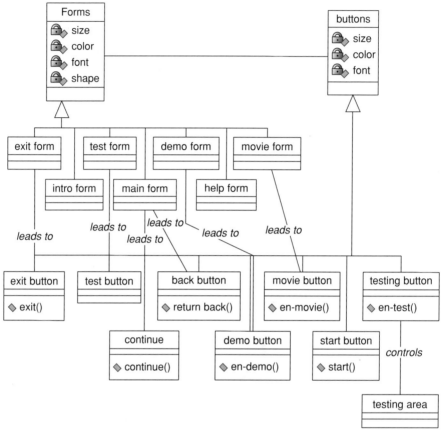

Figure 5-15. **Robot arm reverse engineering object model**

Exercises

1. a) Determine the initial use case model following the systematic steps of the bridge process.
   b) Compare the resulting model with the model in Figure 5-1.

2. Section 2 suggested a rewriting of the three scenarios provided in that section.
   a) Rewrite the scenarios of Section 2, abstracting the commonalties into new scenarios, and describe additional scenarios that you might find appropriate for using the application.
   b) Give the activity diagrams for the scenarios of part a.
   c) Redraw a version of the use case model based on parts a and b. Rely on use relations to capture resulting subscenarios.

3. a) Determine all the objects from Description 5-1 by first selecting the names then deleting those that do not represent objects.
   b) Determine associations by selecting all verb phrases in Description 5-1 and then keeping those that are appropriate to objects reached in part a.
   c) Draw an object model from the objects and associations in parts a and b. Compare your model to the model in Figure 5-4.

4. a) Trace the activity diagram in Figures 5-2 and 5-3 through the object model in Figure 5-4. Identify useful additional classes or associations.
   b) Adjust the object model in Figure 5-4 with the new additions.

Chapter 6

Math Tutor: *Case Study 4*

This case study was developed following the bridge pro-cess with a simple modification. The description of user requirements is rather simple but it is complemented with a detailed description of all stages that the applica-tion goes through and it proves to be useful in advanced phases of the target system design. The initial use case model is very simple, whereas the second version of the use case model exhibit "uses" relations that are worth examining. The object model exhibits inheritance and aggregation relations. Details of traceability and other details that lead to formation of the models are left as a challenge to the reader in the exercise section at the end of the chapter.

1. INCEPTION

1.1 USER REQUIREMENTS

> *Math tutor is an application that educates and trains students in lower level classes in mathematics. The application supports two levels (medium and high) of competency, where each level contains several stages that students have to complete to move across levels. To move from one level to another, a student has to achieve a certain score. Scores are gained during lessons. Each lesson consists of two parts: practice and an evaluation quiz. The student collects his/her score from the first part of each lesson. Each successful level is followed by a game or song in order to motivate the student.*

Description 6-1. Tutor user requirements

Detailed Description of Stages

When starting the application, the student has two choices:

1. The user chooses to take consecutive lessons. The user will start from the lowest level (level 1) and go consecutively through all the lessons of each of levels 1 and 2. In this case, the user will not receive any prize.

2. The user chooses to practice a lesson. This means that the user will be asked to select a level and to take a lesson related to this level. In this case, the user will be provided with a grade and possibly will win a prize (depending on the grade score).

The two levels offered by the application are described in detail as follows.

LEVEL 1
This level includes very low classes, for ages of 4 to 5 years. In this level, the child is meant to acquire the very simple and basic operations of arithmetic. The mathematics part contains the following:

- Lessons in counting
  Example: count figures and shape.

- Lessons in knowing the simple digits
  Example: identify numbers and pronounce them by passing the mouse over a figure, making the figure pop out, and a voice says the name the number.

- Lessons in sorting numbers and shapes
  <u>Example:</u> extracting objects of a certain shape from a group of different shapes and colors. Also sort numbers according to their values or shapes according to their sizes.

LEVEL 2

This level is more advanced, for ages 6 to 7 years. In this level, the student will become acquainted with basic arithmetic operations. The mathematics part contains the following:

- Lessons in Addition
  Subtraction
  Simple multiplication
  Simple problems
  <u>Examples:</u>
  1. An arithmetic operation is given (drawn) on screen and the student gives the answer either by choosing it from the buttons or punching it on the keyboard.
  2. A simple problem including the above operations is both drawn and spelled and the student responds to it and gives the answer.

1.2 USE CASE MODEL (VERSION 1)

The use case model describes the top-level usage of the system.

Figure 6-1 shows a single actor user for the system. The use case model presents two use cases: Takes consecutive lessons and Chooses to practice. These capture the two alternatives offered by the system.

2. ELABORATION

2.1 REQUIREMENTS ANALYSIS

Observe the following scenarios, which are based on the detailed description of stages of the target system provided earlier in the chapter. Observe the

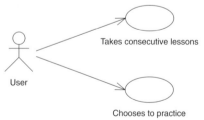

Takes consecutive lessons

User

Chooses to practice

***Figure 6-1.* Tutor use case model**

commonalities between the scenarios that justify the "uses" relation in the second version of the use case model in Figure 6-6.

Primary Scenarios

The following are two primary scenarios. Scenario 6-1 shows a log that permits user to take lessons repeadly. Scenario 6-2 includes a while loop and a conditional part.

1. NAME: TAKES CONSECUTIVE LESSONS *(ACTIVITY DIAGRAM 1)*

Precondition: The user wants to start taking lessons.
1. The user logs into the application.
2. The user chooses "take consecutive lessons."
3. The system launches lesson 1 of level 1.
While the user wants to take a lesson
a) The user follows the instructions.
b) The user answers the questions.
c) The lesson ends.
d) The system returns a grade to the user.
e) The system launches the next lesson.
Postcondition: The user finished taking lessons.

Scenario 6-1

2. NAME: CHOOSES TO PRACTICE *(ACTIVITY DIAGRAM 2)*

Precondition: The user wants to practice a lesson.
1. The user logs into the application.
2. The user chooses "practice a lesson."
3. The user selects the level he/she wants (level 1 or level 2).
4. The user selects the type of lesson he/she wants.
While the user wants to continue practicing
a) The user follows the instructions.
b) The user answers the questions.
c) The lesson ends.
d) The system returns a grade to the user.
e) If the grade is high then
   The user gets a prize (song or game).
f) System launches a harder lesson of the same type.
Postcondition: The user finished taking lessons.

Scenario 6-2

Secondary Scenarios

Name: Running Problems.
Primary Scenario: Takes Consecutive Lessons; Chooses to Practice. The user was not able to run the application.

Name: Incomplete Lesson.
Primary Scenario: Takes Consecutive Lessons; Chooses to Practice. The user interrupted the lesson.

Activity Diagrams

Figures 6-2 and 6-3 show the activity diagrams for Scenarios 6-1 and 6-2. Note the commonality between the activity diagrams in Figures 6-2 and 6-3 that reflects the common activities between the two primary scenarios (Scenarios 6-1 and 6-2).

1. TAKES CONSECUTIVE LESSONS ACTIVITY

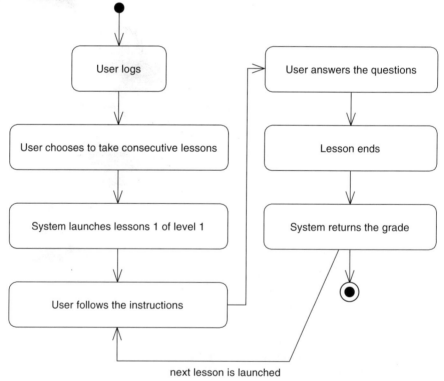

Figure 6-2. **Tutor Takes Consecutive Lessons activity**

2. CHOOSES TO PRACTICE ACTIVITY

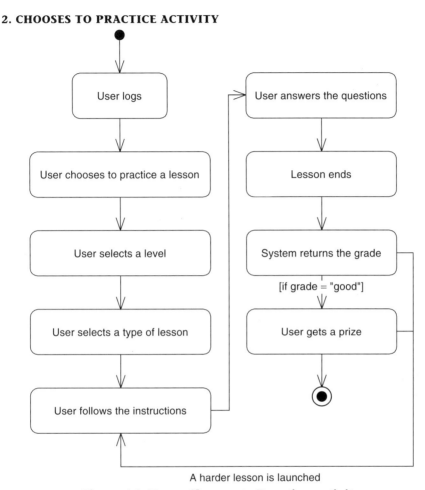

Figure inner labels:

- User logs
- User chooses to practice a lesson
- User selects a level
- User selects a type of lesson
- User follows the instructions
- User answers the questions
- Lesson ends
- System returns the grade
- [if grade = "good"]
- User gets a prize
- A harder lesson is launched

Figure 6-3. **Tutor Chooses to Practice activity**

2.2 DOMAIN ANALYSIS: DERIVING THE INITIAL OBJECT MODEL

Figure 6-4 shows the initial object model. Observe that the model is based on several inheritance relations that are related to the kind of lesson given rather than to the direct usage of the application.

Derivation of the Object Model from the User Requirements

Objects (in Table 6-1) are a subset of names collected from the user requirements in Description 6-1. Similarly associations are a subset of the verb

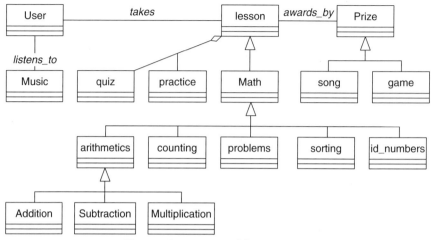

***Figure 6-4.* Tutor object model**

phrases in Description 6-1. The resulting objects and associations are linked together to obtain the object model in Figure 6-4.

DETERMINING THE OBJECTS

From the user requirements and the project description, we have chosen the following objects from the potential names (Table 6-1).

mathematics	lesson	practice	quiz
game	song	User *(student)*	

***Table 6-1.* Objects in user requirements**

Additional object classes were derived from the detailed description of the stages in the application. These are *Counting, Addition, Subtraction, Multiplication,* and *ID_numbers*.

2.3 SOFTWARE SYSTEMS ARCHITECTURE (VERSION 1)

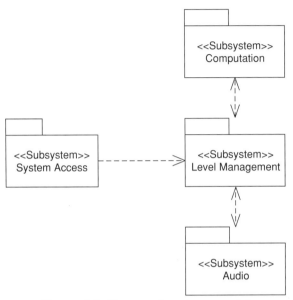

Figure 6-5. Tutor subsystem model

The architecture of the project has been divided into four subsystems that interact with the user, on one hand, and each another, on the other hand. Description 6-2 provides a glossary of each subsystem.

Glossary

1. **System access:** This is the interface package through which the user accesses the system.
2. **Level management:** This is the subsystem responsible for assigning a level to the user and increasing the user level every time he/she improves and gets a good grade.
3. **Computation:** This is the subsystem responsible for all the arithmetic computations displayed to the user, such as addition, subtraction, and multiplication.
4. **Audio:** This subsystem is responsible for managing the sound system in the application, including the music when the user wins a prize or the voice of the application when asking the user to perform some instructions.

Description 6-2. Tutor subsystems description

Derivation of the Subsystems Relation from the Subsystems Description

The aforementioned subsystems communicate as follows. The subsystem **System Access** is accessed by the user. The **Level Management** subsystem interacts with the subsystems **Audio** and **Computation**, because it manages the audio and computation modules. In other words, the **Management** subsystem is the one that decides when the computation process will run and when the audio will run.

2.4 TRACEABILITY

Only the traceability of objects to architectures is summarized (Table 6-2). Tracing the activity diagrams through objects is left to the reader as an exercise.

Objects to Architecture

Object/Class Name	Subsystem Kind
User	System Access Subsystem
Lesson	Level Management Subsystem
Quiz	Level Management Subsystem
Practice	Level Management Subsystem
Prize	Level Management Subsystem
Game	Level Management Subsystem
Math	Computation Subsystem
Arithmetic	Computation Subsystem
Counting	Computation Subsystem
Problems	Computation Subsystem
Sorting	Computation Subsystem
ID_Numbers	Computation Subsystem
Addition	Computation Subsystem
Subtraction	Computation Subsystem
Multiplication	Computation Subsystem
Music	Audio Subsystem
Song	Audio Subsystem

Table 6-2. Mapping of objects to architecture

3. CONSTRUCTION

3.1 USE CASE (VERSION 2)

Figure 6-6 shows the second version of the use case model of the target application. The use case model exhibits a new actor and the introduction of new use cases that are related by "uses" relations.

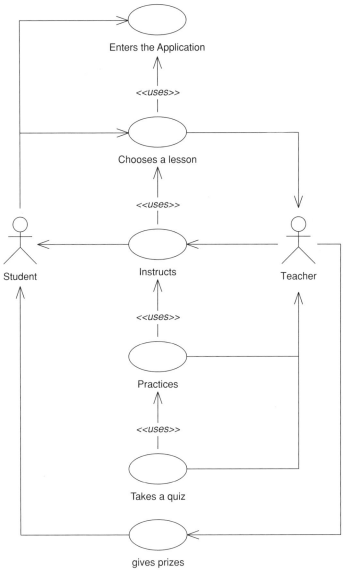

Figure 6-6. **Tutor use case model (version 2)**

Figure 6-6 has two actors, *Student* and *Teacher*. Actor *Student* is introduced because a student is identified to be key user of the application. Actor *Teacher* is introduced because the application acts like a teacher. Hence, we have two new actors **Student** and **Teacher** that interact with the use cases. Additional use cases such as **Enters the Application, Chooses a lesson, Instructs, Takes a quiz**, and **Gives prizes** were introduced in this second version of the use case model mainly as a consequence of the activities that are common to Scenarios 6-1 and 6-2.

3.2 DYNAMIC MODELING: SEQUENCE AND COLLABORATION DIAGRAMS

Only two sequence and collaboration diagrams are introduced that correspond to Scenarios 6-1 and 6-2 introduced earlier (see Figures 6-7 to 6-10).

1. A) TAKES CONSECUTIVE LESSONS SEQUENCE DIAGRAM

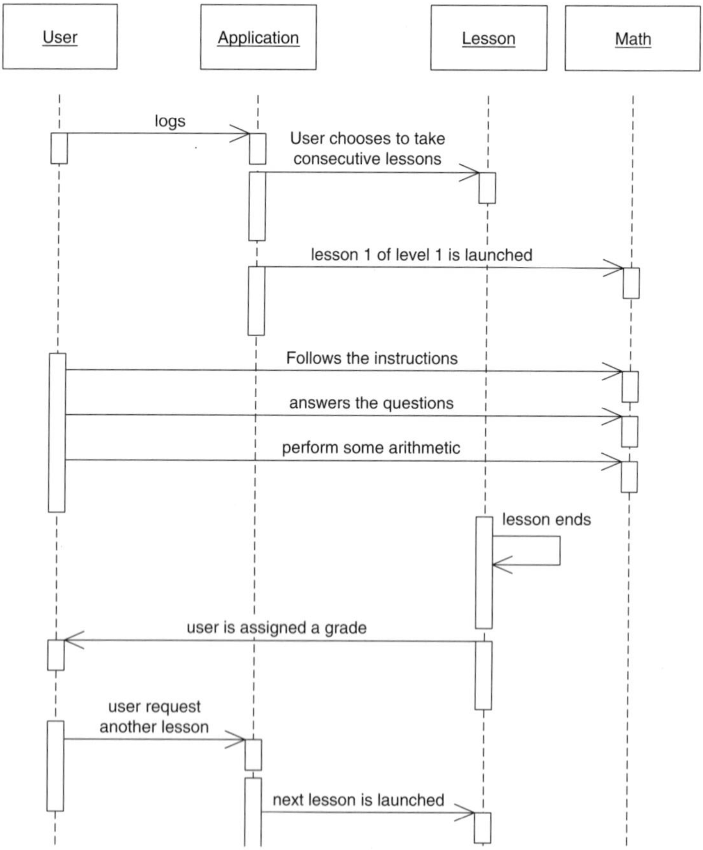

Figure 6-7. **Tutor Takes Consecutive Lessons sequence diagram**

B) TAKES CONSECUTIVE LESSONS COLLABORATION DIAGRAM

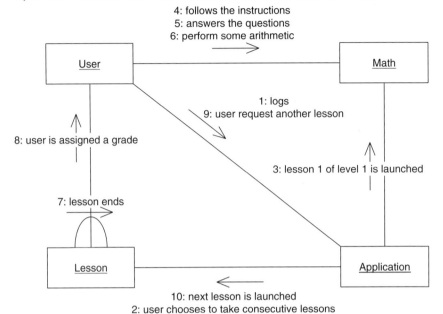

Figure 6-8. **Tutor Takes Consecutive Lessons collaboration diagram**

2. A) CHOOSES TO PRACTICE SEQUENCE DIAGRAM

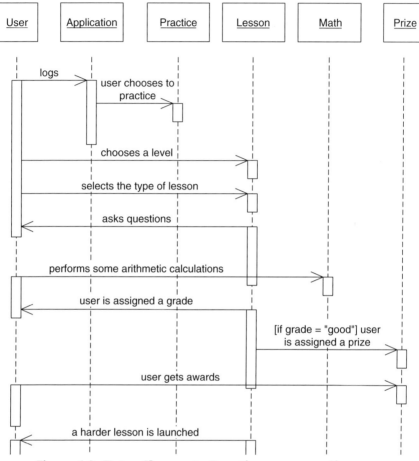

Figure 6-9. **Tutor Chooses to Practice sequence diagram**

B) CHOOSES TO PRACTICE COLLABORATION DIAGRAM

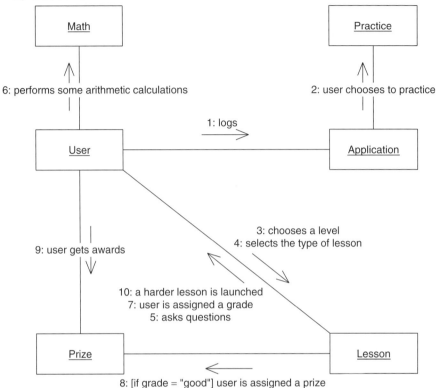

Figure 6-10. **Tutor Chooses to Practice collaboration diagram**

3.3 OBJECT DESIGN

Figure 6-11 shows a detailed version of the initial object (Figure 6-4). The new model contains attributes, new associations among classes, and new additional classes.

By comparison of the object design with the initial object model, we find that the new classes that are added are **software, voice, listener, lesson,** and **instructions**.

Class *Software* captures the application and resembles an entry point to the services – in this case lessons – that it provides. Consequently, it controls and handles communication between the user and the application. Classes *Lesson* and *Instructions* are included from the second version of the use case model; class *Listener* is conceptually and functionally derived from the implementation language. Class *Voice* is an abstraction of classes *Music* and *Instructions*,

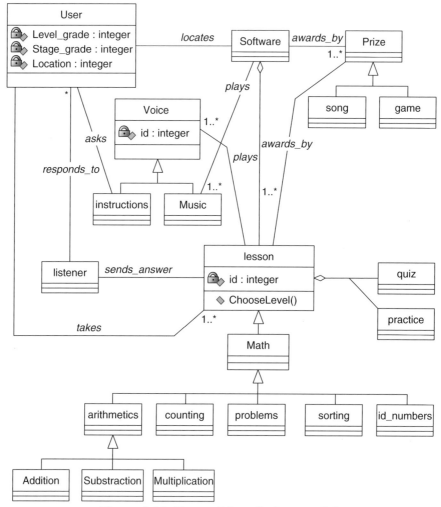

Figure 6-11. **Tutor object design model**

which rely on voice during execution. The new associations are a result of the introduction of new classes and of tracing activity diagrams to the object model. This trace activity is left to the reader as an exercise.

4. CONSTRUCTION/IMPLEMENTATION

The application is implemented in Microsoft Visual Studios Java 1.1. Paint Shop Pro 4.0 was used to create the design interface. The software consists of a concurrent system in which control is distributed among several objects based on a threading approach. The data storage was accomplished via a flat file structure.

Exercises

1. a) Determine the initial use case model following the systematic steps of the bridge process.
   b) Compare the resulting model with the model in Figure 6-1.

2. a) Based on the use case model (version 2), determine and describe additional scenarios for using the application.
   b) Give the activity diagram for the scenarios in part a.

3. a) Determine all the objects from Description 6-1 by first selecting the names and then deleting those that do not represent objects.
   b) Determine associations by selecting all verb phrases in Description 6-1 and then keeping those that are appropriate to objects obtained in part a.
   c) Draw an object model from the objects and associations in parts a and b. Compare your model to the model in Figure 6-4.

4. Visualize the objects traces to architecture summarized in Table 6-2. Can you determine new communication links from the visual model? What are they?

5. a) Trace the activity diagram in Figures 6-2 and 6-3 through the object model in Figure 6-4. Identify useful additional classes or associations.
   b) Adjust the object model in Figure 6-4 with the new additions.
   c) Compare the resulting model in part b with Figure 6-11.

Chapter 7

Distribution Case: Case Study 5

This application focuses on automating the operations of a goods distribution company. The summary of user requirements is appended with all data that may be needed by such applications. Almost all details required by the application are collected from the beginning. The detailed requirements give a useful sample that can be adopted in building similar applications. The activity diagrams depict conditionals and repetitions. Also, the detailed object model is rich with attribute names and associations. The exercises at the end of the chapter lead the user in carrying traceability and other activities that were dropped from this case study.

1. INCEPTION

1.1 USER REQUIREMENTS

Description 7-1 gives a brief description of the application.

> *DVC is a software solution for a given company. This company is a reseller of goods. It obtains its products from a vendor, and resells them to a customer. The basic need of the company is a database to store specific information concerning the various vendors, customers, and warehouse,s as well as a product database. In order to make the lives of the employees easier, the software features an easy-to-use interface for the database, which includes interactive forms and graphics. Using the information in the database, the user can access the information in several easy ways, such as browsing and searching.*

Description 7-1. Distribution user requirements

More on User Requirements

The following are detailed requirements of the application. Most of these will be more useful during the design stage and serve to shape the object model.

Customer

COMPANY/CONTACT INFO
- company name
- address
- phone number
- fax number
- e-mail
- website
- contact names
  - owner/CEO
  - purchasing
  - operations

  Each contact listed also has phone number, fax number, e-mail, and personal info.

PURCHASING INFO
- order logs
  Need info on exactly what you want stored in logs, with examples.
  All the logs contain information concerning the order documentation
  for reference purposes. The various logs include the following:
  - history order log:
    order no., date, order value, invoice no., date estimated arrival, time
    to destination (ERA)
  - current order log: same as above
    + current payment status:
      cash against documents
      21–30 days from the date of bill of lading
    + current shipping status:
      customer name, order no., vessel name, ETD, ETA

- total purchase amount year-to-date (YTD):
  total value of orders from the beginning of the year to date

- total purchase amount, lifetime:
  total value of the orders from the beginning of the company

Vendor

COMPANY/CONTACT INFO
- company name
- address
- phone number
- fax number
- e-mail
- website
- contact names
  - owner/CEO
  - sales
  - shipping
  each contact listed also has phone number, fax number, e-mail, and
  personal info

ORDERING INFO
- order logs
  All the logs contain information concerning the order documentation
  for reference purposes. The various logs include the following:

- o   history order log:
     order no., date, order value, supplier invoice no., date estimated
     delivery time
- o   current order log: same as above
     +   current payment status: net 30 days
     +   current shipping status:
          order no., estimated delivery time, vessel name, ETD, ETA

- total purchase amount, YTD: total value of orders from the beginning
  of the year to date.

- total purchase amount, lifetime:
  total value of the orders from the beginning of the relationship with
  the vendor to date.

Product

PRODUCT INFO
- Products code: a serial number

- Vendor code, if applicable

- Manufacturer code, if applicable

- Brand: this is the brand name

PRODUCT DESCRIPTION/DIMENSIONS
What are the choices you'd like to offer while entering packing detail?

- packing: detail how product is packed inside carton
  no. of pieces in a carton (unit) × net wt of each pieces
  Example: 100 × 9 grams

- net wt: the net weight of the carton in pounds
  the total net wt of a carton (unit)
  Example: 9 kilograms

- gross wt: the gross weight of the carton in pounds
  total gross weight of a carton
  Example: 9.98 kilograms

- cube: the volume of the carton in cubic feet
  Example: 0.516 cft

- what date format do you use, dd/mm/yyyy?
  Example: March 22, 1999

- shelf life: for product dating
  month/year
  Example: 3/1999

PRODUCT PRICING
What sort of magnitude are we looking at here, tons?

> This could be in tons but most frequently in no. of cases. Example: 1,350 cases per a 20-ft container, total estimated volume from this vendor to the company per year, about 40 containers

- min: the minimum quantity that should be ordered from the manufacturer at one time
  This varies from one supplier to the other on the company's product list (Copy is attached; we will add a column to show the minimum order quantity from each item.)

- price: selling price to the customer
  What does FOB stand for? FOB stands for free on board – the correct term should be ex-works – then another cost is added for inland transportation from the works of the vendor to either the warehouse or to the port of shipment of the goods.

- cost: the cost of the product FOB plant
  It is the cost of each case of a product while still at the works of the vendor's location or plant but loaded on the transportation means that will be provided by the company.

- handling: the cost of the inland freight, labeling, and storage, needed to discuss the following relationship, and what equations are used

- relationship between selling price and cost: should be related by a % margin that may vary on the same item from one customer to another

- relationship between selling price and handling: The relationship should be between the cost price and handling. It will be added to the cost in order to arrive to the total cost.

- relationship between selling price and gross wt: no direct relationship

- relationship between selling price and cube: no direct relationship

Warehouse

WAREHOUSE INFO
- warehouse name

- address

- contact info

PRODUCT INFO
- product inventory: This should be as per the attached product list from which you can copy the required info.
  - 2 columns:
    - + Quantity
    - + Specification
      - – Production Date (P) – applicable to food
      - – Expiration Date (E) – applicable to food
    - + Type of storage required (refrigeration – R, frozen – F, dry – D)
    - + Current month
    - + Previous month
  - relation = product

1.2 USE CASE MODEL (VERSION 1)

Figure 7.1 shows version 1 of the Use Case Model. It includes four actors: *Employee, Customer, Vendor, and Warehouse.* Also, it has five different use cases.

Actors

Employee – workers that will access the application.
Customer – client that company sells to.
Vendor – client that company purchases from.
Warehouse – client that company stores in.

Determining Use Cases

Use cases are determined based on why actors would access features of different systems: Order Management, Product Database, Customer Database, Vendor Database, and Warehouse Database (see Figure 7-1).

2. ELABORATION

2.1 REQUIREMENTS ANALYSIS

This phase involves determination of primary and secondary scenarios, then expressing these in terms of activity diagrams.

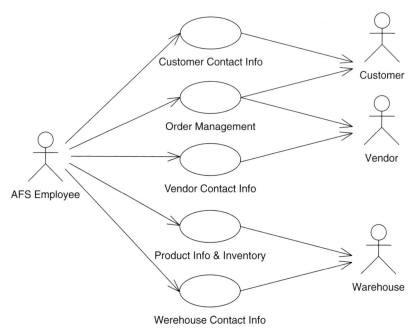

***Figure 7-1.* Distribution use case model**

Primary Scenarios

The following are five different scenarios in which a user can access the system. The scenarios include conditionals expressed in terms of statements that express how the system would branch based on a condition (see Scenarios 7-1 to 7-5). It might be worth noting the similarities in structure and functions of the described scenarios and considering possibilities for rewriting these in terms of subscenarios (see the exercises at the end of this chapter).

1. NAME: ORDER MANAGEMENT (*ACTIVITY DIAGRAM 1*)

Precondition: Order selected on Main Menu
1. Order selected on Main Menu.
2. While the user has not canceled, the software loops.
3. If the user selects Enter New Order then
   Use New Order.
4. If the user selects Browse Orders then
   Use Browse Orders.
5. If the user selects Search Orders then
   Use Search Orders.
6. The user will select a function
   End while.
7. The use case ends.
8. New Order
   a) The user selects Enter New Order from the Main Menu.
   b) The user enters common order information.
   c) The user is prompted to select for which existing customer the order is being placed.
   d) The user is then prompted to specify sales order details by filling out the displayed form.
   e) The user then selects the existing vendor from the contact database.
   f) The user is then prompted to enter purachse order details.
   g) The user then goes back to the Main Menu.
9. Browse Orders
   a) The user selects Browse Orders from the Main Menu.
   b) The user navigates through the Orders.
   c) The user has the option to delete any given Order.
   d) The user then goes back to the Main Menu.
10. Search Orders
    a) The user selects Search Orders from the Main Menu.
    b) The user enters the name of the customer or vendor.
    c) The results appear.
    d) The user has the option to delete the given Order.
    e) The user then goes back to the Main Menu.
Postcondition: User either retrieves info from Order database, enters a new order, deletes an existing order, or cancels and returns to the Main Menu.

Scenario 7-1

2. NAME: CUSTOMER CONTACT INFO (*ACTIVITY DIAGRAM 2*)

Precondition: Customer selected on Main Menu.
1. Customer selected on Main Menu.
2. While the user has not canceled, repeat
   If the user selects Enter New Customer then
     Use New Customer.
   If the user selects Browse Customers then
     Use Browse Customers.
   If the user selects Search Customers then
     Use Search Customers.
   The user will select a function.
   End while
3. The use case ends.
4. New Customer
   a) The user selects Enter New Customer from the Main Menu.
   b) The user enters common order information.
   c) The user enters Customer purchase details.
   d) The user enter Employee details.
   e) The user then goes back to the Main Menu.
5. Browse Orders
   a) The user selects Browse Customers from the Main Menu.
   b) The user navigates through the Customers.
   c) The user has the option to delete any given Customer.
   d) The user then goes back to the Main Menu.
6. Search Orders
   a) The user selects Search Customers from the Main Menu.
   b) The user enters the name of the customer or vendor.
   c) The results appear.
   d) The user has the option to delete the given Customer.
   e) The user then goes back to the Main Menu.
Postcondition: User either retrieves info from Customer database, enters a new customer, deletes an existing customer, or cancels and returns to the Main Menu.

Scenario 7-2

3. NAME: VENDOR CONTACT INFO (*ACTIVITY DIAGRAM 3*)

Precondition: Vendor selected on Main Menu.
1. Vendor selected on Main Menu.
2. While the user has not canceled, repeat
    If the user selects Enter New Vendor then
    Use New Vendor.
    If the user selects Browse Vendor then
    Use Browse Vendor.
    If the user selects Search Vendor then
    Use Search Vendor.
    The user will select a function.
    End while.
3. The use case ends.
4. New Vendor
    a) The user selects Enter New Vendor from the Main Menu.
    b) The user enters common order information.
    c) The user enters Vendor purchase details.
    d) The user enter Employee details.
    e) The user then goes back to the Main Menu.
5. Browse Vendor
    a) The user selects Browse Customers from the Main Menu.
    b) The user navigates through the Vendor.
    c) The user has the option to delete any given Vendor.
    d) The user then goes back to the Main Menu.
6. Search Vendor
    a) The user selects Search Vendor from the Main Menu.
    b) The user enters the name of the Vendor.
    c) The results appear.
    d) The user has the option to delete the given Vendor.
    e) The user then goes back to the Main Menu.

Postcondition: User either retrieves info from Vendor database, enters a new vendor, deletes an existing vendor, or cancels and returns to the Main Menu.

Scenario 7-3

4. NAME: PRODUCT INFO (*ACTIVITY DIAGRAM 4*)

Precondition: Vendor selected on Main Menu.

1. Product selected on Main Menu.
2. While the user has not canceled, repeat
   If the user selects Enter New Product then
   Use New Product.
   If the user selects Browse Product then
   Use Browse Product.
   If the user selects Search Product then
   Use Search Product.
   The user will select a function.
   End while.
3. The use case ends.
4. New Product
   a) The user selects Enter New Product from the Main Menu.
   b) The user enters Product details.
   c) The user then goes back to the Main Menu.
5. Browse Product
   a) The user selects Browse Product from the Main Menu.
   b) The user navigates through the Products.
   c) The user has the option to delete any given Product.
   d) The user then goes back to the Main Menu.
6. Search Product
   a) The user selects Search Product from the Main Menu.
   b) The user enters the code of the Product.
   c) The results appear.
   d) The user has the option to delete the given Product.
   e) The user then goes back to the Main Menu.

Postcondition: User either retrieves info from Product database, enters a new Product, deletes an existing Product, or cancels and returns to the Main Menu.

Scenario 7-4

5. NAME: DELETE YOUR HOME PAGE (*ACTIVITY DIAGRAM 5*)

Precondition: Warehouse selected on Main Menu.
1. Warehouse selected on Main Menu.
2. While the user has not canceled, repeat
    If the user selects Enter New Warehouse then
    Use New Warehouse.
    If the user selects Browse Warehouse then
    Use Browse Warehouse.
    If the user selects Search Warehouse then
    Use Search Warehouse.
    The user will select a function.
   End while.
3. The use case ends.
4. New Warehouse
    a) The user selects Enter New Warehouse from the Main Menu.
    b) The user enters common contact information.
    c) The user enters Warehouse inventory details.
    d) The user enters Employee details.
    e) The user then goes back to the Main Menu.
5. Browse Warehouse
    a) The user selects Browse Warehouse from the Main Menu.
    b) The user navigates through the Warehouse.
    c) The user has the option to delete any given Warehouse.
    d) The user then goes back to the Main Menu.
6. Search Warehouse
    a) The user selects Search Warehouse from the Main Menu.
    b) The user enters the name of the Warehouse.
    c) The results appear.
    d) The user has the option to delete the given Warehouse.
    e) The user then goes back to the Main Menu.

Postcondition: User either retrieves info from Warehouse database, enters a new Warehouse, deletes an existing Warehouse, or cancels and returns to the Main Menu.

Scenario 7-5

Secondary Scenarios

Two secondary scenarios that apply to almost all the previous primary scenarios are as follows:

Invalid data entered

Search not found

Activity Diagrams

Figures 7-2 to 7-6 show the activity diagrams that correspond to Scenarios 7-1 to 7-5. The activity diagrams demonstrate selection and repetition as well as the possibility of an activity terminating in more than one final state.

1. ORDER MANAGEMENT ACTIVITY

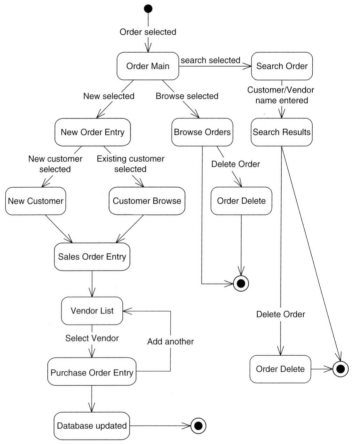

***Figure 7-2.* Distribution Order Management activity**

2. CUSTOMER CONTACT INFO ACTIVITY

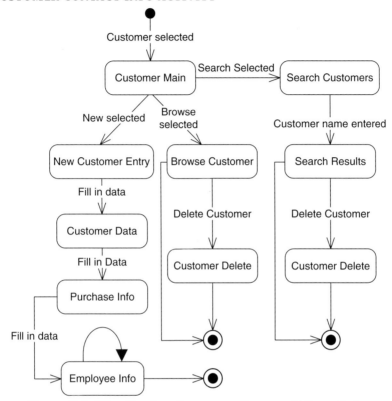

Figure 7-3. **Distribution Customer Contact Info activity**

3. VENDOR CONTACT INFO ACTIVITY

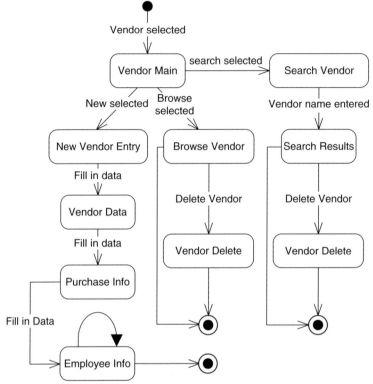

Figure 7-4. **Distribution Vendor Contact Info activity**

4. PRODUCT INFO ACTIVITY

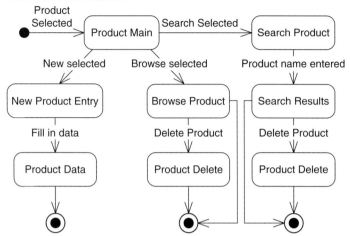

***Figure 7-5.* Distribution Product Info activity**

5. WAREHOUSE CONTACT INFO ACTIVITY

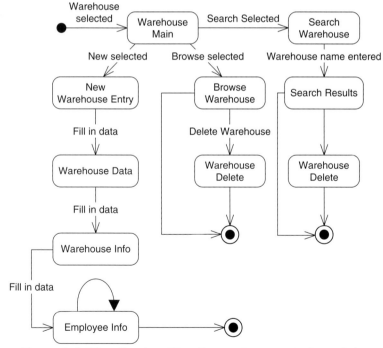

***Figure 7-6.* Distribution Warehouse Contact Info activity**

2.2 DOMAIN ANALYSIS: DERIVING THE INITIAL OBJECT MODEL

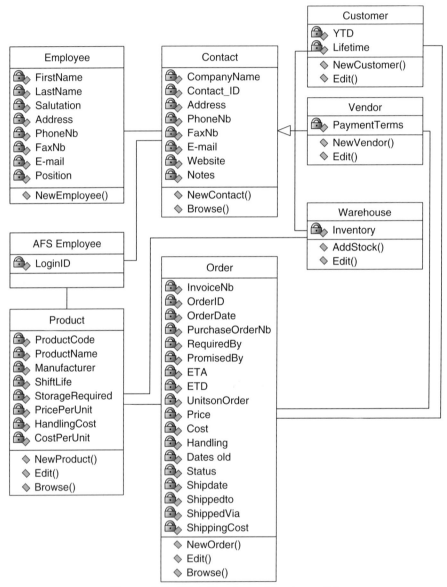

***Figure 7-7*. Distribution object model**

The bulk of the application is made up of the two classes *Order* and *Product* (see Figure 7-7). Class *Order* captures all details of an order that could be placed by a customer, vendor, or the warehouse, which is controlled by employees of the company. Class *Product* is an abstraction of data on all possible products that a warehouse could hold. Clearly, class *Product* could be specialized to account for products that may need special functionality or data. Subclassing is used to allow class *Contact* to capture all contact details that may be required to contact a *customer, vendor,* or the *warehouse.*

2.3 SOFTWARE SYSTEMS ARCHITECTURE (VERSION 1)

MAIN SUBSYSTEMS: CONTACT, PRODUCT, ORDER

Order communicates with Vendor, Customer, and Product.

Warehouse communicates with Product.

INTERFACE AMONG SUBSYSTEMS
Each subsystem is interfaced via its main class. For example, Customer is interfaced via Customer Main, Product via Product Main. Each Main allows the functionality of adding, searching, browsing, and deleting.

DERIVATION OF SUBSYSTEMS
The preceding subsystems were obtained directly from the user requirements as well as the initial class design. Once the various components were clearly identified, selecting subsystems was straightforward.

2.4 TRACEABILITY

This section gives a summary of some trace activities between use cases, objects, and architecture.

2.4.1 Use Cases to Objects
Table 7-1 summarizes the trace activity of Scenario 7-1 of the use case: Order Management to the initial object model in Figure 7-7. All new resulting associations are modeled in bold and italics. The trace activities of scenarios 7-2 to 7-5 are left as exercises.

1. NAME: ORDER MANAGEMENT (*ACTIVITY DIAGRAM 1*)

Step in Scenario	Association	Supplier Object	Client Object
1	Select	Employee	Main Menu
2	Select	Employee	Main Menu
3	New Order	Employee	Order
4	Browse Order	Employee	Order
5	Search Order	Employee	Order
8	New Order		
8 (ii)	Enter Order	Employee	Order
8 (iii)	Select Customer	Order	Customer
8(v)	Select Vendor	Order	Vendor
9	Browse Navigates Delete	Order	Order
10			
10(l)	Search		
Employee	1	Employee	Contact

Table 7-1. **Mapping of use cases to associations in object model**

2.4.2 Objects to Architecture

Table 7-2 summarizes the trace activity of objects in the initial object model to subsystems reached in Section 2.3.

Object/Class Name	Subsystem Kind
Customer	Contact Subsystem
Vendor	Contact Subsystem
Warehouse	Contact Subsystem
Product	Product Subsystem
Order	Order Subsystem
Sales Order	Order Subsystem
Purchase Order	Order Subsystem
Employee	Contact Subsystem
AFS Employee	User Subsystem

Table 7-2. **Mapping of objects to architecture**

3. CONSTRUCTION

3.1 USE CASE (VERSION 2)

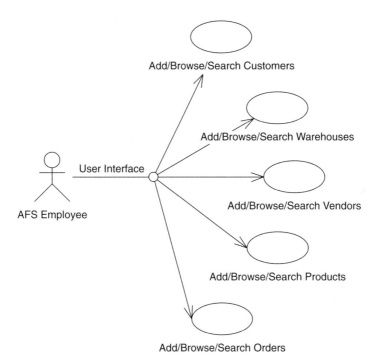

Figure 7-8. **Distribution use case model (version 2)**

Figure 7-8 gives a second version of the use case model of Figure 7-1. Clearly the activity diagrams of the previous section could help in extending the model with useful activities and uses cases. The exercise section covers this part.

3.2 DYNAMIC MODELING: SEQUENCE AND COLLABORATION DIAGRAMS

Figures 7-9 to 7-18 give the sequence and collaboration diagrams for Scenarios 7-1 to 7-5.

1. A) ORDER MANAGEMENT SEQUENCE DIAGRAM

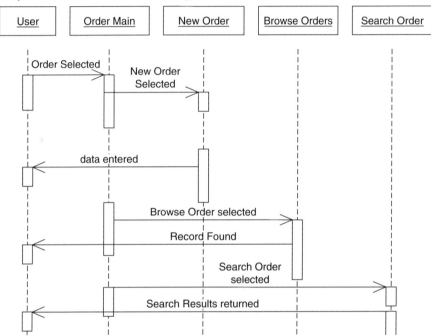

Figure 7-9. **Distribution Order Management sequence diagram**

B) ORDER MANAGEMENT COLLABORATION DIAGRAM

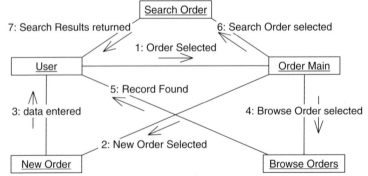

Figure 7-10. **Distribution Order Management collaboration diagram**

2. A) CUSTOMER CONTACT INFO SEQUENCE DIAGRAM

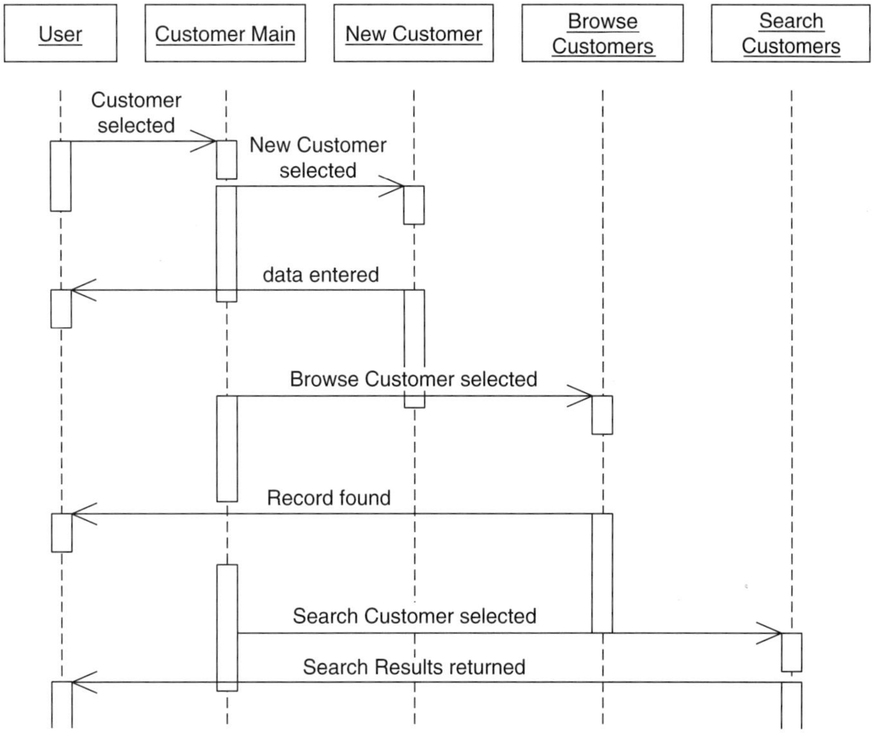

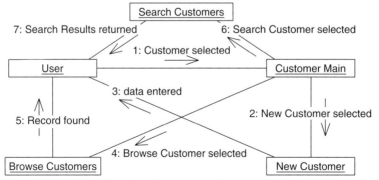

Figure 7-11. Distribution Customer Contact Info sequence diagram

B) CUSTOMER CONTACT INFO COLLABORATION DIAGRAM

Figure 7-12. Distribution Customer Contact Info collaboration diagram

3. A) VENDOR CONTACT INFO SEQUENCE DIAGRAM

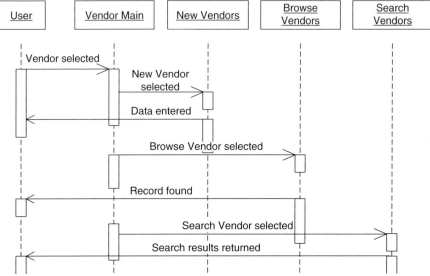

Figure 7-13. **Distribution Vendor Contact Info sequence diagram**

B) VENDOR CONTACT INFO COLLABORATION DIAGRAM

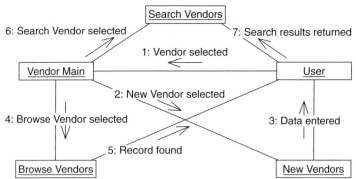

Figure 7-14. **Distribution Vendor Contact Info collaboration diagram**

4. A) PRODUCT INFO SEQUENCE DIAGRAM

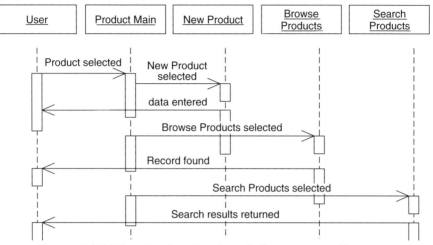

Figure 7-15. Distribution Product Info sequence diagram

B) PRODUCT INFO COLLABORATION DIAGRAM

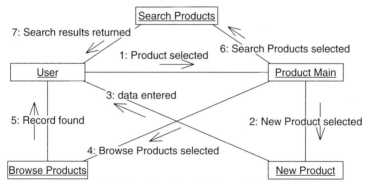

Figure 7-16. Distribution Product Info collaboration diagram

5. A) WAREHOUSE CONTACT INFO SEQUENCE DIAGRAM

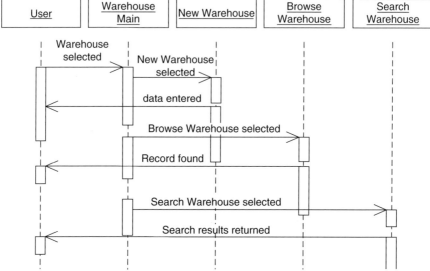

***Figure 7-17.* Distribution Warehouse Contact Info sequence diagram**

B) WAREHOUSE CONTACT INFO COLLABORATION DIAGRAM

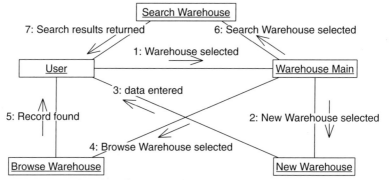

***Figure 7-18.* Distribution Warehouse Contact Info collaboration diagram**

3.3 OBJECT DESIGN

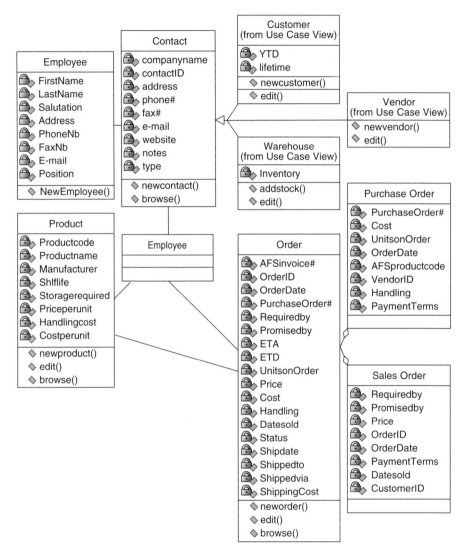

Figure 7-19. Distribution object design model

The object model in Figure 7-19 includes all possible details on the application in terms of additional attributes and functions. In comparison to the model in Figure 7-7, there are two additional classes that specialize orders: *Purchase Order* and *Sales Order*.

234 UML by Example

Exercises

1. a) Determine the initial use case model following the systematic steps of the bridge process.
   b) Compare the resulting model with the model in Figure 7-1.

2. a) Rewrite the scenarios in Section 2.1 to capture similarities in subscenarios. Also determine and describe any additional scenarios that you might find appropriate for using the application.
   b) Give the activity diagram for the scenarios of part a.

3. The object models in Figures 7-7 and 7-19 lack multiplicity and names for the associations among its classes. Modify the model to include these.

4. Determine use case model version 3 from use case model version 2 and the activity diagrams of Section 2.1. Add interfaces where you find these useful.

5. a) Trace Scenarios 7-2 to 7-5 and corresponding activity diagrams in Figures 7-3 and 7-6 through the object model in Figure 7-7. Identify useful additional classes or associations.
   b) Adjust the object model in Figure 7-7 with the new additions.
   c) Compare the resulting model in part b with Figure 7-19.

6. Draw the subsystems model and show all communications among the subsystems.

Appendix A

Recommended Practice

The following is a collection of user requirements, each of which describes the required behavior of a system. Except where otherwise specified for each of the requirements, apply the bridge process to reach a full-fledged design in terms of a use case model, object model, and subsystem model. Apply traceability at all stages.

1. WEDDING LIST

A software for a wedding agency provides a gift reservation facility for couples who would like to have a wedding list, and a gift purchase facility for people who would like to send gifts. The software keeps information on couples and their corresponding wedding lists. Users can access the system to create or update, cancel, view their own wedding list, or to buy certain items from a specific wedding list. Users can also get help on how to use the system without the trouble of contacting employees at the wedding agency. Employees at the agency will administrate the system operations. Employees can delete, update, or add items to inventory. Any complaints or suggestions that the client may have could be sent to the agency and stored in a complaint database. To ensure secure access to the system couples and employees have personal logins and passwords.

   a. Give the actors.

   b. Define the use cases.

   c. Find the objects and describe the interactions between the objects.

   d. Give primary and secondary scenarios for the use cases. Then draw for each primary scenario a corresponding activity diagram.

2. INSURANCE COMPANY

An insurance company wants to automate its functions. The company sells several kinds of insurance policies, including life insurance and car insurance, and has plans to expand its services. Customers can purchase insurance policies, pay insurance fees accordingly, and notify the insurance company of accidents and damages and receive compensation. A customer may purchase more than one insurance policy.

The company has insurance sales persons who market its products to customers and receive claims from customers about accidents and damages. Each insurance plan purchase activity is done through a contract expressed in a written document and results in issuing receipts for payments in installments. Claim adjusters are in charge of handling claims; they study the claims received against insurance plans and issue receipts for compensation purposes. The insurance company has an evaluation procedure to evaluate the productivity of sales personnel and the worthiness of insurance policies against damage claims. For this purpose, the company keeps statistics about customers, insurance policies, and damages.

The system will be built in two phases. Phase I will assume centralization of documents. Phase II will allow Internet connectivity and allow remote online purchasing of insurance plans and document transmission.

   a. Using UML notation give a use case diagram for the insurance system. Briefly describe your use case diagram giving justification to your choice of the actors and use cases.

   b. Consider the following scenario.
     Name: Signing an insurance item.
- The scenario is started by an insurance customer.
- Information about the customer is entered.
- Type of insurance is entered.
- Information about the insurance object is entered. Depending on type of insurance, the appropriate information is included.

- The system calculates the monthly fees.
- A preliminary insurance number, fee, and insurance date are returned to the customer.

1. Give an activity diagram for the scenario just described.
2. Assuming phase I only, derive an initial object model systematically from user requirements. Include multiplicity and constraints if applicable.
3. Give a subsystem model of the insurance system. Justify your choice of the subsystems.

3. CAR RENTAL

The software for the car rental company is supposed to provide online car reservation facilities for people interested in reserving online. So, the application keeps track of all the cars it has and their descriptions. The user can visit the site and can search for a car with certain characteristics. The user is allowed to reserve a car (with or without driver) only if he/she has a valid login to access the system. The customer has to register to obtain a valid login. The customer can also cancel a previously made reservation if it is still possible. The application keeps track of the history of the customers, so each customer can see the cars he/she reserved. The application takes into consideration people who cannot reserve online so the employees are responsible for updating the user account when his/her request is made offline via phone, fax, or even e-mail. The customers are allowed to send feedback to the company regarding its services. The employees have to be able to update the status of the cars they have, add or remove cars, and add or remove drivers. They also have to evaluate customers: this evaluation will be used later for statistics and permissions purposes. Exiting the system is a must after all the processes are done.

1. Identify the actors and use cases and derive the use case model.
2. Construct an activity model for the following primary scenario.
   Name: Search
   Precondition: The user chooses search.
   - The system provides the user with dropdown menus to specify search criteria.
   - The user enters values for the required fields.
   - The user selects submit.
   - User can perform an additional search.

- If User is registered:
  - o   User can make choices according to search.
  - o   Else User chooses to register.
  - o   Else User Exits.

  Postcondition: User has obtained search result.

1. Show how the object model was derived from the previous steps. Draw all the traceability diagrams.

4. AUTOMATED LIBRARY SYSTEM

The public library in the city has decided to go online and, hence, to reach its potential customers everywhere in town. The customers will be able to register online for a monthly fee of $10. They will be able to search for a specific book using a highly developed fast search engine. In case they find the book, they can check if it is available or not. If the book is available, the customer can reserve it for a period of two days in order to go to the library and borrow the book. A customer will be allowed to borrow at most three books at the same time for a period of 20 days at most in order to allow other customers to have the chance to get the books. In case the customer does not have access to the Internet, he/she can still drop by the library and search for his/her books there. In this case, the librarian will provide assistance and update the information on the system whenever a book is taken or returned.

5. FOOTBALL WORLD

The football world is one with the fewest web sites that offer the user the opportunity to browse all football news in the fastest, most reliable means. The page can be easily browsed to view games held, upcoming games, scores, teams lists, players' information, contracts, and much more. The user even has the chance to subscribe as a member of the Football Fan's Club through which he/she gets a daily e-mail concerning everything new or coming soon in the world of football. However, the user may never be allowed to change, update, or delete the contents of the page. That is the responsibility of the administrator(s) of the page who can be identified by a special username/password pair given to him/her in advance.

6. JOB RECRUITMENT

A job recruitment agency decides to go online and increase its line of business. The web page will provide the job seeker with a list of potential jobs to choose from. The job seeker can also post his CV on the web page so that a company searching for new employees can access it easily. The web page will also provide the job seeker with some important tips about what to do and what not to do in the different stages of the job search, such as how to write a good CV, how to search for your match job, and what to wear in the interview. The web page will also provide a search engine for both the company and the job seeker to narrow his/her search based on a minimum salary, type of work, and the country location. In addition, the application will be able to provide a best match between what the user wants and what is available for the moment.

Derive the design model starting from the use case model.

7. HOTEL RESERVATION

Inspired by the online reservation design, try to come up with user requirements for a hotel reservation system wherein a customer can reserve a single, double, or suite through the web for a specific period of time. Include the possibility that a customer can choose to rent a car while reserving a room.

8. RECYCLING MACHINE

Worry about the increasing Green Peace political movement, the government is concerned with finding a solution regarding environment-damaging cans, crates, and bottles. Hence, the government has decided to design a recycling machine that will take care of these items and reduce the pollution in the environment. The citizens will be held responsible for delivering their items to the recycling factory and will get a receipt in return. An operator in the factory will be responsible for counting the number of items delivered per day; filling the recycling machine with the cans, bottles, and crates; and resetting the machine after every use. At the end of each day, the employee will provide the ministry of environment with a summary of the activity of the day, which will be validated and sent to the Green Peace office.

9. BANKING SYSTEM

A bank wants to keep track of its stocks and bonds trading profit using software. The application will store the daily purchase or sale of securities, the sale/purchase price, and the name of the customer. In addition, it will store the commission paid by each customer for each transaction and the brokerage fee that the bank pays to its different brokerage houses. The application will also compute the gain from each transaction as follows:

Gain = Gain from Selling/Buying + Commission – Brokerage.

In order to skip complicated computations, assume that the Gain from Selling/Buying is a positive number stored in the application database.

The system should be able to compute the number of transactions per month, the total gain per month, and the average sale/purchase per day.

Bibliography

Albir, Si Sinan, UML in a Nutshell, O'Reilly, 1988.

Booch, Grady, Object-Oriented Analysis and Design, Addison-Wesley, 1994.

Booch, Grady, Jacobson, Ivar, and Rumbaugh, James, The Unified Modeling Language User Guide, Object Technology Series, Addison-Wesley, 1999.

Brown, David, Object Oriented Analysis, John Wiley & Sons, 1997.

Buschman, F., Meunier, R., Rohnert, H., Sommerlad, P., and Stal, M., Pattern-Oriented Software Architecture: A System of Patterns, John Wiley & Sons, 1998.

Coad, Peter, and Yourdon, Edward, Object-Oriented Analysis, Yourdon Press, 1991b.

Cook, Steve, and John, Daniel, Designing Object Systems, Prentice Hall, 1994.

Eriksson, H., and Penker, M., UML Toolkit, John Wiley & Sons, 1998.

Fayad, E. Mohamad, Schmidt, C. Douglas, and Johnson, E. Ralph, Building Application Frameworks, Wiley, 1998.

Graham, Ian, Object Oriented Methods, Addison-Wesley, 1994.

Jacobson, Ivar, Object-Oriented Software Engineering: A Use Case Driven Approach, Addison-Wesley, 1992.

Jacobson, Ivar, Booch, Grady, and Rumbaugh, James, The Unified Software Development Process, Object Technology Series, Addison-Wesley, 1999.

Pressman, S. Roger, Software Engineering: A Practitioner's Approach, McGraw-Hill International, 1997.

Quatrani, Terry, Visual Modeling with Rational Rose and UML, Object Technology Series, Addison-Wesley, 1998.

Sallis, Philip, Tate, Graham, and McDonell, Stephen, Software Engineering: Practice Management, Addison-Wesley, 1995.

Schach, R. Stephen, Software Engineering with JAVA, The Mirror Higher Education Group, 1997.

Schach, R. Stephen, Classical and Object-Oriented Software Engineering, McGraw-Hill, 1999.

Schneider, G., and Winters, J. P., Applying Use Cases: A Practical Guide, Object Technology Series, Addison-Wesley, 1998.

Sodhi, Jag, and Sodhi, Prince, Object-Oriented Methods for Software Development, McGraw Hill, 1996.

Sommerville, Ian, Software Engineering, Addison-Wesley, 1992.

Texel, P. Putnam, and Williams, B. Charles, Use Cases Combined with BOOCH, OMT UML, Prentice Hall, 1997.

Wilkie, George, Object-Oriented Software Engineering, Addison-Wesley, 1993.

Index

A

active actors, 5
activity diagrams, 25–30
  branching in, 26
  in bridge process, 60–62, 67, 69
  constraints in, 26–27
  in distribution case study, 220–223
  looping in, 27–28, 62
  in math tutor case study, 196–197
  notation in, 25, 62, 104
  in reservations online case study, 90–95,
    104–108
  in robot arm simulation case study, 177–180
  of simultaneous states, 27–30
  in web page maker case study, 137–141,
    149–156
actors, 3
  active *vs.* passive, 5
  communication relation of, 11–12
  in distribution case study, 213
  generalization among, 5–7
  glossaries of, 58, 86, 133
  identifying, 56–57
  names of, 65 (*see also* name selection)
  in reservations online case study, 84–85
  stick-person notation for, 3–4
  in web page maker case study, 131–132,
    133

aggregation associations, 35
aggregations, 35–36, 38, 74–75
algorithm design, 78–79
alternative scenarios, 23–25 (*see also* secondary
  scenarios)
analysis phase, 48–49 (*see also* user
  requirements)
architecture, 45
  in distribution case study, 225
  examples of, 45–47
  in math tutor case study, 199–200
  physical, 128–129
  in reservations online case study, 101–103,
    111–113, 124–125, 128–129
  in robot arm simulation case study, 182–183
  subsystem analysis and, 66–67
  traceability models and, 70, 77–78
  in web page maker case study, 147–148,
    154–156, 165
associations, 34–35
  aggregations, 35–36, 38, 74–75
  communicate relationship, 11–12
  in construction phase, 72–74
  in domain analysis, 65
  in reservations online case study, 97–100,
    108–110
  in web page maker case study, 143–146,
    153–154

ATM machine software, 12, 43–45
attributes, 30
  classes with, 32
  in construction phase, 72–74
  in domain analysis, 66
  in reservations online case study, 100–101
  in web page maker case study, 146–147

B
banking system exercise, 239–240
bank machine software, 12, 43–45
boat purchase example, 9
bookstore inventory system, 10–12, 41–44
branching, in activity diagrams, 26
bridge process, 48–79
  activity diagrams in, 25–30, 62
  construction subphase 1, 70–78
  construction subphase 2, 78–79
  deliverables from, 51, 53–54, 59, 63
  domain analysis in, 63–66
  elaboration phase in, 49, 50–52, 58–70
  glossaries in, 58
  inception phase, 49, 50–52, 53–58
  interfaces in, 45, 63
  overview of, 50–53
  primary scenarios in, 61
  requirements analysis in, 59–63
  secondary scenarios in, 62
  subsystem analysis in, 66–67
  traceability in, 67–70, 77–78
  use case model in, 56–58, 62–63
  user requirements in, 48–49, 53–54, 55–56

C
car rental software, 5, 31, 237–238
CGI interface, 143, 149
chat system software (*see* online chat system software)
classes, 30
  actors and, 3
  aggregations, 35–36
  associations, 34–35
  with attributes, 32
  database, 121–123
  data structure, 120
  examples of, 31, 38–40
  generalization relation, 36–40
  with operations, 32–33
  ordinary, 156
  parameterized, 33–34
  self-association of, 35

  subsystems of, 45
  template for, 31
collaboration diagrams, 42–45
  in bridge process, 42–45, 71, 76–77
  design from, 76–77
  in distribution case study, 228–232
  in math tutor case study, 203, 205
  in reservations online case study, 114–120
  in robot arm simulation case study, 185–188
  in web page maker case study, 158–163
combination, inheritance and, 37
communicate relationship, 11–12 (*see also* associations)
computer board game software, 16–17
computer systems, activity diagram for, 30
constraints, 26–27, 83–84
construction phase, 70–78 (*see also* implementation phase)
  algorithm design, 78–79
  in bridge process, 49, 50–52, 70–78
  detailed object design, 71–77, 120–124, 188–189, 205–206, 233
  dynamic modeling in, 71 (*see also* dynamic modeling)
  in math tutor case study, 201–206
  nonfunctional requirements in, 75–76
  object implementation, 78 (*see also* implementation phase)
  in online reservations case study, 113–124
  in robot arm simulation case study, 184–188
  traceability in, 77–78 (*see also* traceability)
  use cases in, 70–71 (*see also* use case models)
  in web page maker case study, 157–166
consulting company subsystem model, 46–47
customer contact information, 209–210, 216, 221, 229

D
data fields, 32
deliverables
  of bridge process, 51, 53
  of domain analysis, 63
  of the elaboration phase, 59
  of the inception phase, 54
deployment, 128–129
design phase, 50–52 (*see also* construction phase)
  algorithm design, 78–79
  in bridge process, 49, 50–52
  in distribution case study, 233
  in domain analysis, 63–66
  in math tutor case study, 205–206

in reservations online case study, 120–124
reverse engineering model in, 125–127
in robot arm simulation case study,
188–191
in web page maker case study, 157–166
diagrams (*see* activity diagrams; collaboration
diagrams; sequence diagrams)
discrete approach, 49–50
distribution case study, 208–234
activity diagrams, 220–223
architecture, 225
object design, 233
primary scenarios, 214–219
secondary scenarios, 220
sequence and collaboration diagrams,
228–232
traceability, 225–226
use case model, 213, 227
user requirements, 209–213
domain analysis, 63–66
associations in, 65
attributes in, 66
in distribution case study, 224–225
in math tutor case study, 197–199
objects in, 64–65
in reservations online case study, 95–101
in robot arm simulation case study, 180–181
in web page maker case study, 141–147
drawings, robot arm, 174
dynamic modeling, 71
in distribution case study, 228–232
in math tutor case study, 202–205
in reservations online case study, 114–120
in robot arm simulation case study,
185–188
in web page maker case study, 158–163

E
elaboration phase, 58–70
in bridge process, 49, 50–52, 58–70
in distribution case study, 213–226
domain analysis in, 63–66
in math tutor case study, 194–200
requirements analysis in, 59–63
in reservations online case study,
87–113
in robot arm simulation case study,
175–183
subsystem analysis in, 66–67
traceability in, 67–70
in web page maker case study, 133–156
end states, 25
error messages, 23–24
in distribution case study, 220

in reservations online case study, 89–90
in robot arm simulation case study, 177
in web page maker case study, 136–137
extend relationship, 9–10, 15–16

F
financial market persons model, 38
finishing simultaneously, 30
flight reservation system software, 35–36
football world exercise, 238

G
GDPro software, 125, 127
generalization
among actors, 5–7
between classes, 36–40
joke-teller software example, 38, 40
school data base example, 38–39
template for, 37
glossaries, 58
of actors, 58, 86, 133
of classes, 112
of subsystems, 102, 148, 156, 182, 199
of technical terms, 173
goods distribution case study (*see* distribution
case study)

H
Help activity, 175, 177–178, 185
home page creation (*see* web page maker case
study)
hotel reservation exercise, 239
HTML interface, 143, 148–149

I
if statements, 21–22
implementation phase, 49, 52, 78
inheritance and, 37
in math tutor case study, 206–207
in reservations online case study, 124–129
in robot arm simulation case study,
188–191
in web page maker case study, 166–167
inception phase, 53–58
in bridge process, 49, 50–52, 53–58
in distribution case study, 209–213
in math tutor case study, 193–194
in reservations online case study, 83–84
in robot arm simulation case study, 172–175
in web page maker case study, 130–133
inheritance
extend relationship and, 10
generalization and, 5, 36–40
in object model, 72

insurance company exercise, 236–237
interfaces
    architecture of, 45
    in bridge process, 45, 63
    CGI, 143, 149
    HTML, 143, 148–149
    in reservations online case study, 125–126
    in use case models, 17–19, 63
    user, 18
interior designer software, 12, 14
"invalid password", 24
"is" verb, 144
iteration, 26, 40, 49–51

J
job recruitment exercise, 238–239
joke-teller system, 38, 40

L
library system software, 31–34, 238
looping, 22–23, 27–28, 62

M
many-to-many associations, 35–36,
    73–74
mapping
    in distribution case study, 226
    in math tutor case study, 200
    in reservations online case study, 109–111
    in robot arm case study, 183
    in web page maker case study, 153–155
math tutor case study, 192–207
    architecture, 199–200
    domain analysis, 197–199
    implementation, 206–207
    requirements analysis, 194–197
    sequence and collaboration diagrams,
        202–205
    traceability, 200
    use case model, 194, 201–202
    user requirements, 193–194
message passing notation, 40
message returns, 40–41
methods, 30, 32–33
military officer's organization software,
    20–24
"missing data" scenario, 24
music player software, 12, 13

N
name selection
    in bridge process, 65
    in reservations online case study, 84–85,
        96–97

in web page maker case study, 131,
    142–143
notation
    in activity diagrams, 25, 62, 104
    in sequence diagrams, 39–40
    of states, 25
    stick-person, 3–4
    in traceability models, 68
"not registered" scenario, 24

O
object implementation, 78
object models
    in bridge process, 53, 63–66, 69,
        77
    detailed object design, 71–77, 120–124,
        188–189, 205–206, 233
    in distribution case study, 224–225
    in math tutor case study, 197–199
    in reservations online case study, 95–101,
        104–113, 120–127
    reverse engineering models, 125–127,
        190
    in robot arm simulation case study,
        180–181, 190
    in web page maker case study, 141–147,
        164–166
objects, 30–31
    determining, 96–97, 142–143
    in domain analysis, 64–65
    names of, 65, 84, 96–97, 142–143
one-to-many associations, 34, 72–73
one-to-one associations, 34, 72
online chat system software
    activity diagrams for, 25–26
    self-association in, 35
    use case model in, 13–14
    use cases in, 7–8
online reservations (*see* reservations online
    case study)
operations, classes with, 32–33
output interface, 18

P
Page Maker example (*see* web page maker case
    study)
parameterized classes, 33–34
parent–descendant relation (*see* inheritance)
passive actors, 5
password-based transactions, 26–27
postconditions, 20–21 (*see also* primary
    scenarios)
preconditions, 19–21, 61 (*see also* primary
    scenarios)

primary scenarios, 19–22
  in bridge process, 19–22, 61, 63
  in construction phase, 71
  in distribution case study, 214–219
  with if statements, 21–22
  in math tutor case study, 195
  in reservations online case study, 87–95
  in robot arm simulation case study,
    175–176
  typical format in, 20
  in web page maker case study, 134–136
  with while loop statements, 22–23
process models, 48–50 (*see also* bridge process)
product information, 211–212, 218, 223,
    231
property-buying example, 41–43

R
real estate software
  actors in, 4
  primary scenario in, 21
  property-buying example, 41–43
  secondary scenario in, 24
  use cases in, 7–8
recycling machine exercise, 239
rental car software, 5, 31, 237–238
requirements analysis, 59–63 (*see also* user
    requirements)
  in distribution case study, 213–223
  in math tutor case study, 194–197
  in reservations online case study, 87–95
  in robot arm simulation case study,
    175–180
reseller company software, 4, 14–15
reservations online case study,
    83–129
  deployment and physical architecture,
    128–129
  design model summary, 125–126
  domain analysis, 95–101
  interface of main classes, 125–126
  object design, 120–124
  requirements analysis, 87–95
  reverse engineering model, 125–127
  sequence and collaboration diagrams,
    114–120
  software systems architecture, 101–103,
    124–125
  subsystem model, 124–125
  traceability, 103–113
  use case model, 84–87, 113–114
  user requirements, 83–84
reverse engineering models, 125–127,
    190

robot arm simulation case study,
    171–191
  activity diagrams, 177–180
  architecture, 182–183
  domain analysis, 180–181
  implementation, 188–191
  object design, 188
  requirements analysis, 175–180
  sequence and collaboration diagrams,
    185–188
  traceability, 183
  use case model, 174–175, 184
  user requirements, 172–174

S
school administration software, 15–16 (*see also*
    university registration software)
school database, 38–39 (*see also* university
    probation software)
secondary scenarios, 22–25
  in bridge process, 22–25, 62–63
  in distribution case study, 220
  examples of, 23–25
  in math tutor case study, 196
  in reservations online case study, 89–90
  in robot arm simulation case study,
    177
  in web page maker case study,
    136–137
self-association, 35
sequence diagrams, 39–43
  in bookstore inventory example, 41–42
  in buying a property example, 42–43
  in construction phase, 71
  design from, 76–77
  in distribution case study, 228–232
  in math tutor case study, 202, 204
  notation in, 39–40
  in reservations online case study,
    114–120
  in robot arm simulation case study,
    185–188
  in web page maker case study, 158–163
sharing, inheritance and, 37
simultaneous states, 27–30
site ordering software, 45–46
software company model, 37
software systems architecture (*see* architecture)
specialization relationship, 5, 37
star topology, 128
start states, 25
states, 25, 27–30, 62
state transition diagrams (*see* activity
    diagrams)

subsystems, 66–67
  architecture of, 45, 128
  communication among, 103
  database, 128
  in distribution case study, 225
  glossaries of, 102, 148, 156, 182, 199
  in math tutor case study, 199–200
  in reservations online case study, 101–103,
    111–113, 124–125
  in robot arm simulation case study,
    182–183
  in web page maker case study, 147–148,
    155–156, 166
system architecture (*see* architecture)

T
television watching software, 28–29
Test activity, 176, 180, 187–188
testing phase, 49
"time response error", 24
Tours Online case study (*see* reservations
    online case study)
traceability, 67–70
  advantages of, 50, 103
  in distribution case study, 225–226
  in math tutor case study, 200
  in reservations online case study, 103–113
  in robot arm simulation case study, 183
  in web page maker case study, 149–156
traces, 67–68
transitions, 25–28, 67
transitivity, in generalization, 36
travel agency software, 76–77 (*see also*
    reservations online case study)
Tutor case study (*see* math tutor case study)

U
university probation software
  activity diagrams in, 27–28
  nonfunctional design requirements,
    75–76
  primary scenario in, 22–23
  user case model in, 18–19
university registration software, 8, 24
university student association software, 76
use case analysis, 68–69 (*see also* domain
    analysis)
use case models, 11–19
  building, 12–15
  communicate relationship in, 11–12
  in construction phase, 70–71
  diagrams of, 58
  in distribution case study, 213, 227
  with extends relationship, 15–16

identifying actors in, 56–57
  in inception phase, 54–55
  with interfaces, 17–19, 63
  in math tutor case study, 194, 201–202
  in requirements analysis, 59–63
  in reservations online case study, 84–87,
    113–114
  in robot arm simulation case study,
    174–175, 184
  with uses relationship, 16–17
  in web page maker case study, 131–133,
    157–158, 165
use cases, 7–11 (*see also* use case models)
  communication relation, 11–12
  examples of, 7–8
  extend relationship between, 9–10, 15–16
  identifying, 57
  notation for, 7
  in reservations online case study, 85–87
  uses relationship between, 10–11, 16–17
  in web page maker case study, 132–133
user interfaces, 18
user requirements, 55–56 (*see also*
    requirements analysis)
  in automated library system example, 238
  in banking system exercise, 239–240
  in bridge process, 48–49, 53–54, 55–56
  in distribution case study, 209–213
  in football world exercise, 238
  in hotel reservation exercise, 239
  in insurance company exercise, 236–237
  in job recruitment exercise, 238–239
  in math tutor case study, 193–194
  in recycling machine exercise, 239
  in rental car exercise, 237–238
  in reservations online case study, 83–84, 98,
    100–101
  in robot arm simulation case study, 172–174
  in web page maker case study, 130–131,
    142–143
  in wedding list exercise, 235–236
users, actors and, 3–4
uses relationship, 10–11, 16–17

V
validation, 49, 52, 58
vendor contact information, 210–211, 217,
    222, 230
verb phrases (*see also* associations; use cases)
  in bridge process, 57, 62, 65
  in reservations online case study, 85, 97–100
  in web page maker case study, 132, 143–146
verification, 49, 52
Visual J++ language, 124–125

W

warehouse information, 212–213, 223, 232
waterfall model, 49
web page maker case study, 130–167
  activity diagrams, 137–141, 149–156
  actors, 131–132
  architecture, 147–148, 154–156
  domain analysis, 141–147
  implementation phase, 166–167
  object design model, 164–166
  primary scenarios, 134–136

requirements analysis, 134–141
secondary scenarios, 136–137
sequence and collaboration diagrams, 158–163
subsystems, 147–148, 166–167
traceability, 149–156
use case model, 131–133, 157–158
user requirements, 130–131
wedding registry example, 56–57, 235–236
while loop statements, 22–23
working simultaneously, 27–29